Medieval Civilization

Medieval Civilization

Formation, Fruition, Finality, and Fall

✦   ✦   ✦

LARRY D. HARWOOD

WIPF & STOCK · Eugene, Oregon

MEDIEVAL CIVILIZATION
Formation, Fruition, Finality, and Fall

Copyright © 2016 Larry D. Harwood. All rights reserved. Except for brief quotations in critical publications or reviews, no part of this book may be reproduced in any manner without prior written permission from the publisher. Write: Permissions, Wipf and Stock Publishers, 199 W. 8th Ave., Suite 3, Eugene, OR 97401.

Wipf & Stock
An Imprint of Wipf and Stock Publishers
199 W. 8th Ave., Suite 3
Eugene, OR 97401

www.wipfandstock.com

ISBN 13: 978-1-4982-3488-7
HB ISBN 13: 978-1-4982-3490-0

Cataloging-in-Publication data:

Harwood, Larry D.

Medieval civilization : formation, fruition, finality, and fall / Larry D. Harwood.

xii + 130 p. ; 23 cm. — Includes bibliographical references.

ISBN 13: 978-1-4982-3488-7

1. Civilization, Medieval. 2. Middle Ages. Church history—Middle Ages, 600–1500. I. Title.

BR252 H18 2016

Manufactured in the U.S.A.

For Anna Beth

Historical periods and cultures are invariably many-sided and diverse, and nuance and detail, not gross generalization, are the historian's proper subject. But the historian is also called to the task of synthesis, and his final responsibility, the goal of his craft, is to order the many and shed light on the whole.

—STEVEN OZMENT

Contents

Preface | ix
Acknowledgments | xi

Chapter 1. The Classical World and
Christian Beginnings, 323 BC–AD 33 | 1
    The Athenian Empire Eclipsed | 1
    Hellenism to the Ends of the Earth | 4
    The Mystery Religions | 8
    The Christian Story | 10
    A Mystery Religion in the Roman Empire | 13

Chapter 2. The Ascending Christian Religion, 33–313 | 16
    The Significance of Jesus | 16
    Christian Inroads into the Jewish World | 19
    Christian Inroads into the Roman World | 22
    Jewish and Christian Futures | 24
    Christian Expectations and Organization of the Christian Church | 26

Chapter 3. Formation of Medieval Civilization, 313–814 | 31
    Christianity after Constantine | 31
    Christianity after the Roman Empire | 36
    East and West | 40
    The Rise of Islam | 42
    Establishing the Roman Church | 45

Chapter 4. Fruits of the Burgeoning Medieval Civilization, 814–1054 | 49
    Charlemagne | 49
    After the Carolingians | 51

CONTENTS

    Monasticism Grows | 55
    Reformers and Marauders | 59
    Christian Advance and Split | 61

Chapter 5. From the Heights of Medieval Civilization, 1054–1347 | 66
    Gregorian Reform and Medieval Exuberance | 66
    New Critics, New Orders, New Learning | 70
    New Heresies | 75
    Rise of the Universities and Controversy over Aristotle | 76
    Rise of Nationalism and the Vernacular | 80

Chapter 6. Fall and Descent of Medieval Civilization, 1347–1517 | 84
    The Black Death | 84
    The Advance of Mysticism | 86
    Social and Theological Criticism of the Church | 89
    New Worlds Discovered, the Jews Considered, and the Word Reconsidered | 91
    Medieval Implosions and Explosions: Science, Weaponry, and the Turks | 94

Chapter 7. The Medieval Legacy, 1517–1648 | 100
    Protestant Reformations | 100
    The Protracted English Reformation | 108
    The Catholic Reformation and the Wars of Religion | 115
    The End of the Middle Ages | 123

Select Bibliography | 127

Preface

The Middle Ages are mysterious to most modern people and maybe offensive to more. A reader who knows a bit about the age—particularly something eliciting negative opprobrium, such as the Inquisition—may be so dismissive as to suggest that the age was sunk into a cauldron of darkness that only the emergence of modernity extinguished. A study of the cultural values of the Middle Ages from this perspective is therefore as likely as not to serve as a catalogue of the history of errors from which, thankfully, we have extricated ourselves as modern people. Gross stupidity, unimaginable superstition, and incalculable cruelty are apt to be epithets attached to this age. Continuing in this same vein of interpretation of the age, some would contend that each of these descriptions are consequences of the Middle Ages being a time in which religion and its henchmen were in charge of the world. Therefore what medieval people believed and did is precisely what we should expect of anything or anybody associated with religion. In this kind of criticism, there is little mystery at all to the Middle Ages, only the muddle of a world gone wrong because the wrong people and wrong institutions and wrong beliefs carried the day for about a thousand years. The only glee that could attach itself to a consideration of the Middle Ages is a thankfulness that the whole sordid age is over.

Readers with such a perspective on this age are not likely to take up a book on the Middle Ages at all, so actual readers may question the reason for a reference to a perspective regarding the age as only and supremely vile. However, the view spoken of is certainly present and carries significant clout in our day. In the pages that follow I certainly do not intend to suggest that those knowledgeable of the era will love the Middle Ages and everything about the Middle Ages. However, a thousand-year spread of history is worthy of more than a few tart or sarcastic epithets condemning it to oblivion.

Preface

One can hardly understand aspects of the modern world without some understanding of the world beforehand. Nor can one understand the history of the world or the history of a civilization, culture, nation, or empire while neglecting some exposure to the religious tradition or culture that the culture was built around. A modern reader who is familiar with and part of a world that is significantly secular or religiously indifferent can easily underestimate the importance of religion in prior human history. At the same time, a recognition that the Middle Ages of the Western world are tied closely to religion can make a modern and secular reader feel that the Middle Ages are alien to him. They are, and in a study of the Middle Ages he should encounter some of the many differences between himself and the past from which his present came.

For such reasons, I make no apology for religion as a predominant theme in the pages of this brief work on the Western Middle Ages. Perhaps more of an apology is necessary for succumbing to the vice of the historian who feels it incumbent to explain one age by a prior age and that age by the age prior to it. Being aware of the cumulative extension of human history, the historian finds it difficult to start and stop his recounting of the past because he realizes that historical sequences will be violated by absolute starting and stopping points. Partly for this reason, the first two chapters of this book and the last chapter attempt to provide some bridges to the opening and closing of the subject of the Middle Ages. For readers who finds this excessive or too much to read, they can concentrate on the four middle chapters of the book where the span of the Middle Ages proper is presented.

—Larry D. Harwood
La Crosse, Wisconsin

Acknowledgments

To my wife Dottie, I owe many thanks for always listening to my stories about the Middle Ages. Thanks are especially due to her for having immeasurably sparked my interest in history. I shall always be grateful to her for her inspiration and for her unflagging support of me in writing this book.

With sincere gratitude I thank Dr. Glena Temple, VP for Academic Affairs at Viterbo University, for her unwavering and always helpful support. To my department head, Dr. Bill Reese, I owe hearty thanks for his patience and for infinite kindness extended to a department member whose projects were not always predictable.

To Judy Ulland, I wish to convey my utmost thanks for having read the entire manuscript of this book meticulously. She made many helpful suggestions. Her aid and encouragement have been extremely valuable to me in this project and others.

1

The Classical World and Christian Beginnings, 323 BC–AD 33

THE ATHENIAN EMPIRE ECLIPSED

In the year 399 BC, an Athenian jury sentenced the able philosopher Socrates to death. That event was a culmination of a quarter century of wearying tumult within the Greek world and followed on the heels of raging warfare between the two most famous of the many Greek city-states at that time, namely Sparta and Athens. The full force of animosity among rival and neighboring Greeks, though common, was occasionally subdued in order to unite against a hated enemy such as the Persian Empire to the East, but now wrath fell mightily against Athens when even the Persians came to aid Sparta in the fight against Athens.

With Pericles (495–429 BC) as the head of the Athenian city-state, Athens had earlier built some architectural marvels, such as the Acropolis and Parthenon, topped off by a majestic statue of Athena, the patron-goddess of the Athenians. The finances for these costly projects were provided by Athenian trade exports such as olives and pottery. Abundant trade had made Athens into something of an international nexus for buyers and sellers who found it a lucrative place. Its budding democracy permitted an extraordinary and historically unique exchange of ideas that made Athens a center for thinkers immortalized in the history of thought. However, even with such marks of cultural vitality and dazzling wealth on display, Athens, under Pericles, was hardly at peace, for Sparta presented a perpetual menace to Athens. In festering anxiety, Pericles decided on a plan and made a case to his citizens that Athens would be wiser to strike first at Sparta than to wait on the eventual and inevitable strike on Athens. However, though Pericles secured permission from those Athenians possessing the right to vote, once begun, the hoped-for brief conflict turned into a meandering and protracted war of almost three decades, known as the Peloponnesian Wars. Sparta was the victor in 405 BC. In part, Athens lost the conflict because plague had decimated an Athenian population crowded too close behind city walls, and because a Spartan alliance with Persia supplied Persian money for building a Spartan naval fleet to finish off the lingering Athenian resistance. The Spartan terms of defeat were harsh, and Athens sustained great humiliation with little prospect for return to former glories. In this gloomy context, the Athenian authorities sought to undertake some overture of fault-finding and thus provide some understanding for such unmitigated disaster. Socrates, though patriotic, was also a perpetual questioner and debater who was brought forward and tried. In his defense, he argued for the rightness of his thinking and actions, and in fearless rebuttal, he laid all sorts of charges at the feet of accusers who held the life of the marked man in their impatient hands.

With Athens defeated, the long war over, and Socrates now dead, the Greek legacy of free-thinking, science, metaphysics, and notions of democratic rule would require other generations of gifted Greeks—most notably Plato (427–347 BC), a student of Socrates, and Aristotle (384–322 BC), a student of Plato. In other words, some of the greatest legacies of the Greeks were about to be built by these thinkers. However, the perpetual stain of what Athens had done to Socrates persisted, with Plato withdrawing from politics and disdaining the democracy judged by him as bearing final responsibility for his great teacher's execution. Aristotle, though a Macedonian, frequented Athens, but on one potentially perilous occasion remarked that he must leave, lest "Athens sin twice against philosophy."

The classical world of antiquity corresponds roughly to the time of greatest achievements of the Greek and Roman Empires. One cannot comprehend the medieval period of Western history without some reference to notable features of these preceding epochs; indeed, not a few of the elements of the later medieval period are prefigured by elements of the Greek and Roman inheritance. This fact requires some knowledge of ways these formative cultures prior to Christianity stamped this religion with indelible marks and provided possibilities for its growth, but of course, too, how Christian and then medieval cultures inaugurate different cultural components compared to the existent Greek and Roman foundations of the Western world.

The Classical World and Christian Beginnings

Alongside these two cultural precursors of the Middle Ages, attention to the mother or predecessor religion of Christianity—that is, Judaism—is also essential. However, Christianity, though thoroughly Jewish in origin, began to swell enormously by incorporating Gentiles or non-Jews into its numbers. Paying particular attention to some details of how the Jewish people interfaced with Greek and Roman culture is necessary, for the nature of these relationships provides some understanding for how Christianity will respond by way of integration or rejection of these traditions. As Christianity grew larger and eventually politically powerful, the daughter religion sometimes persecuted those of Jewish fath in subsequent centuries of the Middle Ages.

With the collapse of a defeated Athenian Empire and much of Greece exhausted by the long conflict between two city states and their allies, the catalyst for extending Greek ways to a larger world would now fall on the Macedonians, the next empire builders after the Athenians, even though Greek neighbors to the south of Macedonia considered these ruffians to be Greeks only by a stretch of the Greek imagination. Nevertheless, Aristotle's most famous student and another Macedonian, the future Alexander the Great (356–323 BC), would eventually assume the helm of Mediterranean power from his father Philip (382–336 BC) and produce an empire beyond any previous imaginings. Interestingly enough, the conqueror Alexander proved to be less provincial than his famous teacher Aristotle. Whereas Alexander welcomed and insisted upon some of his soldiers marrying women of subject populations for purposes of solidifying his conquests, Aristotle, by contrast, had thought of all non-Greeks as barbarians and judged such mingling of these two groups to be ill-advised.

No longer under the tutelage or correction of Aristotle, Alexander would have to submit to his generals when his armies reached India by way of Punjab, for these exhausted men refused to go any further. Alexander's early death at about the age of thirty-two prevented what could have been a united or single empire from ruling such vast domains as Alexander had conquered, though his death did not prevent Greek ideas from permeating these domains. The so-called "Greek mind" of Hellenism promulgated itself into vast regions of the world thereafter. Jewish populations residing far from Jerusalem would be influenced by this Hellenism, though its reception would sometimes create disunity among the Jews. Indeed, one could say that the Jews constituted the single group or culture that opposed Hellenism in significant numbers. This difference, among others, made the Jews a distinct people and suspicious group to many.

HELLENISM TO THE ENDS OF THE EARTH

It is usual to date the beginning of Hellenism around the time of Alexander, who died in 323 BC. By his campaigns in the East, Alexander's political successors would bring elements of the Greek mind to regions where none knew the Greek language or Greek ideas before. In time, moreover, Greek would became the international language of this "new" world; we thus encounter one of the most significant transformations of the known world at that time by the introduction of Hellenism, both in language and ideas. Interestingly, while the spoken language of Jesus three centuries later was Aramaic, the written language of the New Testament, which records his life and teaching, is nevertheless Greek. In other words, even after the pinnacle of classical Greece and its noblest achievements eclipsed, in Hellenism they live on residually as the age introduced much of the surrounding world to Greek ways of life and thinking. This introduction was by no means automatic, for the break-up of Alexander's conquests amongst his generals and their successors required continual maintenance of these conquests, and this task was far from assured. For example, portions of the Seleucid Empire, constituting most of the Asian empire left to Alexander's general Seleucus (c. 358–281 BC), succumbed a half century later to the able Indian leader and Buddhist reformer, Asoka (304–232 BC). Asoka, nevertheless, managed a court and empire that remained open to Greek ideas. Alexander, for his part, had earlier tried to meld something of East and West at the highest level by making the position of Macedonian kingship more akin to the pomp of pharaohs and Persian kings and their extravagant courts. The closeness to emperor worship that this kind of regal culture implied would provoke opposition from some of the Hellenists who saw this kind of veneration as too much departure from a more mellow accord the self-respecting Greeks assumed between themselves and their leaders.

The Greeks, however, tended to favor and assume the identity of the religious and the political. This coalescing gave a kind of ultimate unity to the city-state. This way of thinking, moreover, is implied in one of the charges against Socrates at his trial. He discouraged devotion and worship toward the gods of the Athenians. To his Athenian accusers, this made Socrates a political liability above his other crimes, however much or little these accusers might have believed or disbelieved in the deities of Athens. The Romans would have a similar attitude toward the early Christians who separated the things of God from the things of Caesar, similar to the way the Jews had, and thereby, both incured the wrath of the Romans. This kind of Jewish, and later Christian, division between the sacred and secular irritated Greek and Roman society which shared little of it.

However, though the small and separate Greek city-states still lived on after Alexander, none were so powerful individually as they had been. Alexander dealt them a crushing blow, and the vulnerability of enfeebled individual city-states would prompt alliances between some because of individual weaknesses. With Alexander, the idea of an exalted ruling monarchy became one of elaborate sumptuousness (complete with kowtow), and the territorial monarch became the norm after Alexander's generals began to assume ownership of his foreign conquests, with the Macedonian conquerors ruling over their foreign populations and the dispersion of the ideas of the Greeks among the non-Greek populations assured. The idea of Hellenistic civilization spreading far afield but as a unified enclave of cultures in part depended upon use of the trademark Greek language and variants, for Greek represented Hellenism. Much like the later Western medieval language of scholarship, court, and papacy, that is, Latin, the Greek language and its offshoots provided a nucleus for Hellenism and its extension into the world. To make something approaching a nearly universal culture without an accompanying language that identified Greek ideas and practices would have proved virtually impossible.

It is fairly common among historians to set the end of the age of Hellenism with the Roman victory over the Greeks at the Battle of Actium in 31 BC. This battle was the final defeat of the Ptolemaic kingdom and therefore the end of the previous Hellenistic kingdoms that Alexander's generals had divided up amongst themselves three centuries earlier. As the expansion from Rome begun centuries earlier extended into another empire called the Roman, it is appropriate to see in the rise and civilization of Rome, a successor of Hellenism. Rome had first made acquaintance with the Greeks in the Roman Etruscan past, and it was not long before the Romans undertook to emulate many things Greek. During the Roman republican period and in the amassing of what would eventually be the Roman Empire, the Romans began to see the advantage of conquering the cultures and territories around them. Indeed, before the Christian era, they had made a network of empire second to none in the world of that day, save perhaps the Chinese. Before that, however, they had to beat back the successors of Alexander's generals who hung on tenaciously, particularly in the form of the feared Carthaginians. In the year 202 BC, the Roman general Scipio bested the opposition, though commanded by the notable general, Hannibal. So menacing, however, were the Carthaginians that Roman fears could only be laid to rest in 149 BC, when the third Punic War saw Rome as the victor and the revered but now conquered city of the Carthaginians salted. The Romans were slowly laying their enemies at their feet. However, Rome was no more loved than Greece had been by all its conquered peoples and populations, but those same people could nevertheless often marvel at the industry of the Romans and the kind of order the empire brought to a conglomerate of varied cultures existing within its borders. Later Christian thinkers would ascribe to Roman order, law, roads, language, and other things, indication of divine providence in making for the growth of the Church. When this empire later collapsed, Christian lament was immense, even though in earlier times, the Church frequently suffered persecution at the hands of the Romans.

The Macedonian Empire in some ways prepares the Greek world for the reception of religions significantly alien to the rational motifs of Hellenism, and therefore historians of secular bent have tended to see the Greek mind of Hellenism slowly succumbing to or being usurped by a religious and emotional ethos that will in time erode the previous grandeur of Hellenism. Weighing the years following the death of Alexander the Great in 323 BC usually makes for divisions among these centuries. Historians have been fond of evaluating earlier rather than later decades as the best of Hellenism. This is simply because in part it is closest to the classical period which calls to mind the great contributions of thinkers like Plato and Aristotle, not to mention the great Greek tragedians, playwrights, satirists, and historians. However, even into the latter times of the Hellenistic era, the tendency to rationalize and to seek for the reason in things was still exuberant, though the inroads of skepticism and cynicism and something of a malaise of despair now also appeared. Moreover, for all the unity Hellenistic thinking produced in the world, there was alongside a cosmopolitan mingling of ideas and a considerable diversity of thought. In other words, the march of Hellenism also produced an age of pluralism. Of course, one might note that the classical age was hardly more unified than its successor. That is, we do witness within that age the seething animosity between the Sophists and Socrates and the vastly diverging views among the pre-Socratics on the nature of reality that turned Socrates to consider the smaller questions of the nature of human nature and the like. Even the philosophies of Plato and Aristotle, usually presented in terms of their relatedness, are in fact much more a study in contrasts, even opposite viewpoints. The traditional lumping of these two great thinkers into teacher and student tends to dilute perceptions of their distinctive and multifarious differences.

The thinking of one age compared to another, moreover, should hardly be estimated only by congruence with a predecessor. Such a comparison is hardly a measure of progress; indeed it may be more indicative of stagnation and slavish obedience to one's predecessors. On the other hand, change as change is hardly synonymous with better or worse. Given these kinds of considerations, we might simply assess the age of later Hellenism before the origin of the Christian Church as an age of ripening and cosmopolitan pluralism. We might contend that more open-mindedness starts to prevail, though perhaps to excess in radical skepticism. Nevertheless, Hellenism allowed in some varieties of thinking and religiosity not as close to the thought (or even rigidity) of previous Greek thinkers. One significant and material manifestation of this is the fact of Persian and other Eastern influences upon Hellenism. That is, in going to some of the ends of the known earth of its day, Hellenism most certainly influenced some of these cultures and places, but it too was influenced by them. In indicating this reality, moreover, one may possibly lay at the feet of "Orientalism" responsibility for a Near Eastern religion, Christianity, felling a great Greek and Roman inheritance conceived in rationalism and reason; such is the thesis of the Enlightenment historian of the Roman Empire, Edward Gibbon (1737–1794).

THE MYSTERY RELIGIONS

Acknowledging the cumulative effect of various influences upon Hellenism, not a few scholars have contended that gods and salvation came closer to many humans influenced by Eastern ideas as reason and rationalism weakened in their wake. On the other hand and from another perspective, the so-called mystery religions imported from the East provided for some of the desire for a religious connection deemed muffled or muted in much of the Greek and Roman inheritance by comparison. Undeniably, some of the oriental ideas encountered in this period offered new religious possibilities notably foreign to the Greek mind. Nevertheless, philosophies and religions construed as ways of coping now come into prominence with some grasped as able aids to human life. Even the anti-religious rants of an Epicurus (341–270 BC) are ultimately produced from his desire to form an emboldened emotional life that is not unduly disturbed by upheavals that might challenge or even knock us off our feet. Indeed, the metaphysical heights and some of the finesse of prior Greek philosophy, as we find in Plato and Aristotle, are scaled back in Hellenistic philosophy, and most thinkers now write about morality and ethics; the point is generally how to hold fast in a storm. Sufficiency, even self-sufficiency, is sometimes presented as having the capability of calming the vicissitudes of life.

The so-called mystery religions were more popular at the time than most of the notable philosophers because in part these religions provided something of a story in which humans found a regimen for redemption, however much some critical thinkers would contend that no corresponding enlightenment could be found in these religions—only gross superstitions. However rare though an effort to synthesize both was, a thinker such as Plutarch (c. 46–120 AD) made an attempt to keep some of the traditional Greek and Roman mythology as he purged the unsavory elements. Like Plato on Homer, he refused to take any story as credible that portrayed God or the gods as immoral or fickle. At the same time that he prescribed a serious moralistic religion, he also adhered to belief in the authenticity of oracles, common in much of the past, and to some degree miracles, but as out-workings of divine providence, and not as showy or bizarre spectacles. Plutarch was not alone in his tendency to incorporate the previous

The Classical World and Christian Beginnings

mythologies within moralistic religion, for earlier Cicero (106–43 BC), the Roman senator and orator, had pruned many of the same elements of the previous mythologies. Collectively, moreover, such new and various syntheses seemed to be pointing toward another conception of God and the goals of the religious life. Change seemed in the air.

However, the mystery religions usually went too far for thinkers who judged them by reasonableness and thus required of any purported revelation from deity some credible support. Christianity began to take the lead among the mystery religions of the first century, and by the second century, we encounter Christian apologists arguing against opponents of Christianity. These apologists or defenders of the new religion contend that this religion neither shreds reason nor affirms irrationalism. It is not a primitive and barbarous religion fit only for the unthinking. The charge of cannibalism sometimes leveled against this religion, for example, is a misunderstanding of the nature and purpose of the Christian Eucharist. Thus, the Christian religion found itself in its first decades lumped into the camp of the mystery religions and rarely elevated into the company of curious thinkers. Within some of these mystery religions is evidence of an effort toward the notion of one God, but also oftentimes an acknowledgement of offenses against deity. The perceived need for redemption in time came to figure into such religions rather prominently, and the forms that this need undertook, to critics, often smacked of frothy and unlicensed anthropomorphism, and so seemed closer to a Homeric conception of the world and Homeric gods. To some, this new Christian religion appeared to be a regression rather than a way of advancing thought and civilization. Meanwhile, and as mentioned, thinkers such as Plutarch and Cicero had tried to separate the older and cruder conceptions of the religious life in the interest of maintaining an orderly religious regimen in service to and congruent with a civilized conception of deity and a refined religion. Therefore, by contrast, the mystery religions may not have looked much like anything that officers of the state or empire might desire, but for adherents, they seemed to meet or resonate with a human need requiring more than simply right thinking or rational mythologies. They were therefore popular among the populace, but for the most part impugned by thinkers and officials of the day. Into this world the Christian religion came, and it met with some of the same reaction from powerful quarters that the mystery religions met with, for it was one of them.

THE CHRISTIAN STORY

Plato's spiritual emphases are commonly assumed to be one cultural stepping stone to the success of the Christian message, and it is certainly true that the early centuries of Christian thinking resonate heavily with Platonism. However, Plato's emphasis on the spiritual and non-material world is too removed from the ordinary man to prod him, by reason alone, in the direction of spiritual realities. Moreover, the historical dimensions of Judaism as well as Christianity place both religions virtually immediately in the human historical sphere, and devotees interface with God in the dimension of time, even if God is conceived, as God is in these traditions, as existing outside time. In this historical dimension Judeo-Christian doctrines and ideas have their origin. An idea, for example, is not first developed and some history tacked to it, but rather the reverse. This is what is meant by referring to these religions as historical religions, meaning that they are imbedded within history because they issue from it and are indebted to it as their source. Ideas typically have to be fleshed out to have broader appeal, while religions such as Judaism and Christianity start with flesh so to speak. The book of Genesis starts with the creation of the world and the first humans; the first Gospel of the New Testament starts with the genealogy of Jesus. The realities of the Creation and the Incarnation will be continual sources for conceptualizing these religions, even as these religions begin, we might say, rightly understood, without the conceptions in the beginning.

The practical life demands practical things that may provoke conceptual thinking and conceptual puzzles, but concepts for the sake of themselves will command less attention from the populace than from the philosophers. Within a search for meaning, however dimly or clearly viewed, the seeker wills to find his place and his duty. Therefore, it is not precisely true that pragmatic interests are solely selfish. Rather, the need for something is counterbalanced by need for justification or acceptance or propitiation. The wrath or judgment of God or the gods may play a rather disturbing part to moderns in the earlier aspirant's impetus to seek or placate or appease that being, but the point is simply that the aspirant does not solely come to deity with his hands out, but also with his face down. One might say that mortal man before modernity seeks for that which will provide abiding relief from his plight of offense as well as satisfaction for his need. This is to in effect say that most people are rather utilitarian in regard to the things in their lives, but that they are not solely selfish in this quest.

The Classical World and Christian Beginnings

For as long as Athens was glorious and for as long as later Hellenistic culture managed to give unity to something of a common Greek experience of the world, life provided comfort and even some complacency and perhaps satisfactions for many of the ordinary mortals of the day. The unsettling experiences of later decades when the ascending Romans began to pick away at the empire of the Greeks, however, eroded something of that stability and comfortableness and sent inquirers looking in other and different directions. When the Roman Empire starts to falter later still, some will seek security with it, or away from it, and still others will anticipate some possibilities from it; one Roman Emperor, Constantine, is such a candidate. Political and religious aspirations, the former something at odds for both the Jewish and early Christian culture confronting the Greeks and Romans, will in time find some unity in the Christian Roman state—or the thing called Christendom.

The Christian story is a simple but also a profound story, providing glimpses into the theological complexity of a religion furnishing many of the ideas and much of the framework for the coming Middle Ages. Considering its ascent in the world and the brevity of time in which it is established as a movement with a significant following, the story is a most unlikely one for any historical success at all. Given its humble and rather remote beginnings and the competing religions and ideas of the day, to include the political structures bounding it, one could easily conclude, setting aside our knowledge of its subsequent history, it should have inevitably failed, while earning at the very most a footnote in a general history of the time.

Its bare essentials are the story of a Jewish carpenter, reared in Nazareth of Galilee by humble and devout parents. At adulthood, Jesus—the name given him by his parents on instructions from an angel— takes on twelve disciples, corresponding to the Jewish twelve tribes descending from Jacob, the grandson of Abraham, the latter the most revered figure in Judaism and considered father of the faith in that religion. Jesus, however, beginning at about the age of thirty, clashes with Jewish leaders and not infrequently the people of his day, even as he maintains close adherence to the Jewish traditions and sees himself as the fulfillment of Jewish prophecies. According to the Gospel accounts, Jesus is not so much popular as he is unsettling. Crowds are sometimes ready to honor him and at times, to condemn him; even among the normally almost always hostile leaders, some incidents are recorded where individual influential people come to him privately attempting to size him up in a rather searching and sincere manner.

Jesus's band of disciples have the normal human difficulties of understanding a teacher who presents himself and particularly his mission in the world in terms difficult for them to comprehend. The many exchanges between teacher and disciples recorded in the Gospels reflect the normal ebb and flow of such a relationship, though blended in are the suggestions of Jesus as more than a teacher, both from Jesus and the observing disciples. His disciples are of various occupations; four are fisherman, one a tax collector for the Romans, and one described as a Zealot, meaning engaged in plotting to overthrow the despised Roman yoke around the Jews. Despite the variety of their backgrounds and personalities, after spending three years with him, none possess the courage to go with Jesus to his bitter end of a humiliating trial, beatings and mockings, and then to his crucifixion. In a variety of ways, these followers scatter when disaster falls upon their teacher, presumably as they fear death for themselves if they stay too close. One of them, however, Judas Iscariot, had a significant hand in betraying Jesus, and indicative of the aura surrounding his teacher, this disciple kills himself shortly afterward with unbearable grief over his traitorous actions. The others, moreover, remain fearful because of their association with Jesus, now savagely killed. After a time of grieving and undoubted soul-searching, these hesitant followers would probably have returned to their previous livelihoods, though with frequent and unforgettable episodes of memory dominating the remainder of their lives. With their deaths, their story would probably have sunk down deeply into historical memory and in time, probably would have been forgotten.

However, Jesus's mother Mary and some other women on the morning of the first day of the week make a visit to the burial place, but find no body. Their fuller story gets back to the disciples, who are dismissive of the details provided by the women, but two of them, Peter and John, make their way to the same place and encounter an angel who tells them they are looking in the wrong place for their master who no longer is dead. Now they are not so much fearful anymore, as they are dumbfounded.

The Classical World and Christian Beginnings

Over the next few weeks, the disciples come to believe something that prior to Jesus's death they could not fathom, though he had spoken about it to them on occasion. Their teacher would now be deemed more than simply a profound and spell-binding teacher, and simply not a mere man either, but instead the man whom God sent into the world to endure the very cross and crucifixion that had earlier scattered his frightened followers. Now in a manner of days and then weeks, this same band of initially shattered disciples find extraordinary courage and begin to preach and teach about Jesus as the resurrected Christ and the messiah of the Jewish people and after a while, as the Savior of the world—Gentiles or non-Jews included. However much they have now overcome some of their previous misunderstanding about their teacher, the extension of the message of Christ and redemption to include the whole world, not just the Jewish world, staggers and confounds some of them for a time.

A MYSTERY RELIGION IN THE ROMAN EMPIRE

Visibly present always and everywhere to Christians from the beginning were the Romans, just as they had been for the Jews before Christianity. Initially the Romans seemed to have looked at this new religion, not as precisely a new religion, but simply a sect or offshoot of Judaism, but in time its rather burgeoning numbers from Gentile converts make it cause for potential alarm for some Roman authorities. The word "potential" is used here advisedly to indicate that various Roman authorities had varying attitudes toward such a group. However, one should note that for the Jews and the Christians, their attitude toward Rome was governed by theology, while Rome's attitude toward them was essentially governed by considerations of statecraft. That is, neither Jews nor Christians wanted a political leader or emperor exalting himself as a god-like figure and the Jews expressly did not want political superintendence of their religious affairs. Acts of sacrilege by Roman officials or Roman soldiers were especially galling to the Jews, who would forever remember Pompey the Great's unauthorized entry into the Holy of Holies of the Jewish temple at Jerusalem in 63 BC. Rome, on the other hand, looked with disfavor upon any theology or ideology which viewed Rome's political leaders with disdain bordering on fomenting revolution, such as some in the Jewish population did. In this respect, in the very beginning, the Christian religion probably appeared quite harmless to the empire for it seemed to carry no adversarial political component with its religious message. Indeed, one of the most quoted sentences from the mouth of Jesus for two thousand years has been his answer about who is the rightful recipient of taxes: "Give to Caesar the things that belong to Caesar and to God the things that belong to God."

The Christian message is very soon taken far afield, indeed, within a mere generation, to the capital of the Roman world, the wondrous city of Rome itself. Rather swift persecution in Jerusalem not long after the resurrection of Jesus had sent disciples and followers scurrying for the safety of places from where they could effectively preach their message. Some go far afield, and traces of their extensive journeys are resident in the history of nations such as India, which touts itself as recipient of the Christian message initially carried to that land by the disciple Thomas. The example of Christian communities in India and elsewhere provides needful reminder that the growing Christian religion lurched also eastward in this extension. The new religion certainly did grow in a westerly direction, but from the beginning, Christianity grew rather meteorically in the East.

One might contend with justification that the competition and critique of the mystery religions, along with an insurgent return to Platonism, now called Neo-Platonism, somewhat paradoxically provided Christianity with its opening into the wider world. That is, with the mystery religions, Christianity offered an explicit story of salvation to which the devotee could attach his purpose and his life. In short, Christianity was a practical

The Classical World and Christian Beginnings

religion, not because it gave practitioners things to do per se, but because it gave them a reason to be, seen in light of God's purposes for people. Furthermore, Christianity manifested the reality of bonded community that weathered the vicissitudes of life by mutual support sanctioned by the Christian God's love for humans. Christianity exhibited itself also as a materialistic religion in the sense that God took on flesh in Christ coming into the world. However much ensuing thinkers in coming centuries would try to puzzle out specifics of the God-Man Christ, the founder of this religion had come to humans as one of them. His teaching evidenced much about the relationship between God and humans and about human relationships. One might even say that the metaphysics of Christianity will have to start with the physicality of its origins, its embeddedness in human salvific history, and therefore the humanistic character of the Christian religion partly evokes some of its ethic of humanitarianism.

By contrast, even though Neo-Platonism often supplied Christian intellectuals with a metaphysical conception that could be adapted to the new religion to a significant degree, Platonism skewered the material elements of existence. Therefore, while this component of Platonism was not always easily fitted with the material facets of the Christian story and ethos—and sometimes torturously so—the spiritual focus of Neo-Platonism provided a link to the new religion from this classical tradition of Greek thinking. However, while such a link might provide intellectual respectability to the new religion, the resurgence of Neo-Platonism in the third century most often presented itself as hostile to the new religion. Stunning is the silence of the infamous Plotinus (AD 205–269), who does not even mention the religion in a day in which one could not avoid noticing it. He probably thinks it not of sufficient credibility to provoke comment, even negative comment. Less restrained is his disciple Porphyry (AD 233–304), who charges the Christian conception of the Incarnation as inventing a false notion of the relation of God to the world. The deity of Platonism is hardly commensurate with reference to humans, whereas the Christian notion is that God has not only spoken but has walked among men. This Christian saga, therefore, would provide more attraction to those interested in the mystery religions than to those of a philosophical bent, at least in the beginning.

2

The Ascending Christian Religion, 33–313

THE SIGNIFICANCE OF JESUS

Christian belief, which will be the grand narrative from which much of later medieval history springs, starts with an extraordinary man, deemed a God-Man and referred to most often as Jesus Christ by his followers. Though of humble origins, he does not come into the world without precedent or fanfare, even as he is born in a stable for animals. A star leads both wise men of the East and ordinary shepherds to the stable. Three decades later, a rustic and swarthy Jewish preacher named John the Baptist begins to preach a message of repentance and subsequent baptism before Jesus begins what is usually called his public ministry at about the age of thirty. Indeed, it is Jesus's baptism by John that seems to launch this period of about three years before he is put on trial by adversaries.

It has been difficult for modern historians, starting around the time of the nineteenth century, to put Jesus into plausible perspective, for the winds of belief and unbelief have vacillated such that Jesus is often made into what respective ages presume to see in such a figure. It is commonplace in our day, for example, to tout and extol Jesus's efforts to "change the world," but in Jesus we seem to have a figure who did not have this as his work. Nevertheless, we can observe how much his message did just that, for no man in the history of the world at this or any other time has impacted the world more than this individual. This is not to say, however, that Jesus's message achieved something he did not intend, but rather that the Christian message has often counted his followers in terms of nations and continents and empires. What gave Jesus and his message this kind of power and legacy? It is too facile and deficient to say that his power was in his ethic of, for example, kindness to others, even one's enemies, or turning the other cheek. One can find quite similar admonitions in the pages of Taoism's *Tao Te Ching* or in the sayings of the *Analects*, ascribed to Confucius. Indeed, a perusal of thinkers and men out of other religious and philosophical traditions will reveal a fair amount of similar ethic by way of comparison. In making such comparisons, however, the intent is not to take away from Jesus's most essential or basic message, but to say that it is not precisely this that differentiates Jesus from other great teachers or personages in human history.

At the same time, the most significant point or event about Jesus's life and his teaching is that neither ends with his death. That is, his overturned death gives a particular prominence to his teaching, but the part of his teaching singularly distinctive is how he sees the lives and destinies of human mortals in light of his death and resurrection. Certainly, much of the meaning of the life and death and resurrection of Jesus will elude his followers for some time, even after they encounter the risen Christ. Nevertheless, in contrast to Socrates, for example, Jesus comes into the world to die, not as a depressed, suicidal neurotic or an aspiring revolutionary or a man courageously living by his ethic to his bitter end mocking his accusers, but rather as a man who places his love for humans in the heart of God and who atones for the sufferings due them in his own death. In other words, and though it takes the eventual encounter of the resurrection to instill something of this meaning of Jesus's life and death into his disciples for rumination and then into the sermons of these men, this man comes into the world to take the rightful judgement of a righteous God against unrighteous humans. Perhaps the most notable point about all of this is the evident but extraordinary mercy of a God so astoundingly generous and gracious enough to undertake and accomplish such an act. It is, therefore, not without reason that the Christian story is often referred to as the "greatest story ever told." Partly as an acknowledgement of such mercies, the resurrection of Jesus begins to confer upon his closest followers a courageous willingness to speak of this divine mercy which makes possible human immortality with God because of Christ. Expressed another way, it is not so much what Jesus said—as important as what that is for understanding the man—but what he did. The conveyance of this message sent many disciples to their own crosses as willing martyrs, while their teacher and now Savior had contemplated his cross out of obedience to his calling but with great fear and trepidation for what he must endure in separating himself from God in taking on the sins of men. The human realization, then, of God's purposes in the life and work of Jesus is the catalyst of a telling ministry that, though it sometimes stumbles, presents this message as its reason to proclaim something to the world. Rather than returning to their previous livelihoods, as they might have without belief in this message, these disciples redirect their lives into proclamation of their teacher as the Savior of the nations.

Belief in the resurrection of Christ, however, does not launch the now-convinced followers into precisely immediate action, for some few days later, and after the ascension of Christ to heaven, the Holy Spirit comes upon these disciples as promised in Jerusalem, to the dumbfounded amazement of people gathered around them. Some of the disciples "speak in tongues" and some of the foreigners of the group are stumped upon hearing their native language being spoken. Some account the speakers drunk, but for the disciples, this occasion of Pentecost is sufficient for them to now get out and boldly and fearlessly preach their new message. Peter, therefore, preaches an enthusiastic sermon, with none of the hesitations nor indecision shown weeks before, and the writer of the Acts of the Apostles indicates that at the conclusion of his sermon, about three thousand people were added to the number of disciples.

Though the number of followers continues to increase, the understanding among the various disciples of all that Jesus's life and death and resurrection meant would take some time. Oddly enough, in some cases it could be that someone who had not known Jesus during his earthly life came to a greater understanding of Jesus than the original twelve disciples. Indeed, something of this access to Jesus across time was intimated in Jesus's famous encounter with his disciple known as "doubting Thomas." Before the encounter Thomas had announced to his fellow disciples that he could only believe their contention of a resurrected Christ if he were allowed to insert his fingers in the nail holes of the man he had seen hanging from a cross. When the opportunity to do so presents itself, Thomas retracts his previous stipulations, and instead utters to the risen Jesus, "My Lord and my God." Jesus's response to Thomas's response is to say that Thomas has believed because he has seen, and Jesus adds that equally blessed will be those who will believe without benefit of what Thomas has seen. In other words, the presence of Christ and the indwelling of the Holy Spirit will distribute itself across time and cultures, such that the Christian message has a timeless aspect and virtually limitless possibilities. Said yet another way,

The Ascending Christian Religion

the historical embeddedness and particulars of the Christian story take on a universal validity and timeless applicability to followers.

CHRISTIAN INROADS INTO THE JEWISH WORLD

The rapid rise of Christianity is due in part to the genius of a St. Paul (c. AD 8–68) in positioning himself within the Jewish community coupled with his strategy for appeal to Gentile converts. The intrinsic and long-standing differences between the Jewish lifestyle and that of the Gentiles were so many as to make it appear that any bridge was impossible between the two groups. Nevertheless, as is clear from a reading of the Acts of the Apostles in the New Testament, Paul made it his practice to go to the Jewish synagogue as one of the first things he did in visiting any city. The synagogue as an institution does not appear in the Jewish Old Testament, but reference to it is prolific in the New Testament, in no small part due to cataloging the travels of Paul through his letters to various churches and the chronicling of those travels in the Acts of the Apostles. In all probability, the synagogue was brought into being by Jews who lived far afield of Jerusalem. This extension of Judaism into the wider world was partly a result of previous periods of exile from their homeland, when exiles did not return even when permitted. For others, living away from Israel was simply motivated by opportunities afield which precipitated simply moving and relocating. Collectively, the populations of Jewish communities outside Jerusalem are often referred to as diaspora, meaning dispersed. The synagogues within these dispersed communities provided persons of the Jewish faith a place to worship outside the magnificent temple located in Jerusalem. However, these diaspora Jews were more familiar and in many ways more open to the influences of Hellenism and Greek ways and culture than their brethren in Jerusalem, the Holy City. Moreover, it is indicative of how pervasive Hellenistic modes of life and thought were by the rather constant references to "the Greeks" in the pages of the New Testament. Though Jerusalem and Judea are under the occupation of the Romans and the Roman Empire by the time we come to the Christian New Testament, the predominant cultural competitors with Judaism are still things Greek, with the Romans in charge.

Paul attempts to stand for Christ and between Jew and Greek, though there are obstacles to overcome with each. As he famously writes in his First Letter to the Corinthians, "For Jews demand signs and Greeks seek wisdom, but we preach Christ crucified, a stumbling block to Jews and folly to Gentiles, but to those who are called, both Jews and Greeks, Christ the power of God and the wisdom of God."

Paul therefore had his work cut out for him, though he seems as fearless as Socrates in taking his message to his world, filled as it is with Jews and Greeks, and lest we forget, Romans too, of which Paul is one also. He knows virtually no boundaries, and will take his message to anyone who will listen, dismayed or not, by the particulars of his preaching. One of his most famous ventures is when he goes to Athens, the birthplace of so much of the proud Athenian civilization and where he confronts the Epicurean and Stoic philosophers. His hearers are baffled by some of his ideas and phrases, particularly the notion of the raising of the dead and the resurrection of Christ, but he also quotes from writings from the tradition of some in his audience. The venture is hardly a success, though partially so. More importantly, the effort is indicative of a man with a message that he believes in without reservation wherever he takes that message.

One obstacle to the Jews, though Paul is Jewish also, but now espousing Christ as the redeemer of all people groups and not only Jews, is that the scruples of Jewish diet, proper Sabbath-keeping and many other habits of Jewish identity for centuries, now appeared imperiled by a Christian Gospel that would seem to leave behind these earlier accoutrements for a Christian freed of many of them. Stated so baldly, this notion would be understandably disconcerting or infuriating to a Jew aware of the Jewish centuries of attention to such things which others had often mocked and this Christian variant of Judaism now seemed only too willing to let be gone. However, what was an understandably grievous loss to ponder for most persons of the Jewish faith was an equal if not greater gain to a Gentile or Greek "God-fearer." Such a person would have frequented a Jewish synagogue indicating some desire to associate with that faith. However, many and maybe most of these same persons had flinched under some of the Jewish requirements for full admission to the Jewish faith. Now, however, these previous requirements did not seem to be requirements with the new variant of Judaism seen in the Christian religion. The exodus of these Gentile God-fearers from association with Judaism to membership in the Christian community now seemed apparent. St. Paul seized on this possibility with as much energy as he spent time defending the Christian theological justification for it.

Furthermore, Paul made no pretense to be any better than any of his Jewish brethren; rather, his argument was that he carried the message of

The Ascending Christian Religion

the Jew Jesus who had made him, Saul, a new man, Paul, not because of any merits of the old Saul or merits of the new Paul. Indeed, as Saul, he had actively persecuted the new sect of Christians and participated in the stoning death of Stephen, the first Christian martyr. In other theological wording, Paul appealed to the notion of the Christian as a new creature because he had been redeemed on the cross of Christ by the God who saved him, irrespective of a sordid past. The depravity of the debt of his past and that of others was paid for on the cross of Christ. This was his message, and he and the other disciples and their converts took this message out to the world.

Interestingly, some of the places Paul and others would plant Christian churches were direct descendants of Alexander's conquered lands. Here Hellenism would have been alive and well, in such places as Antioch in Syria and most famously in the proverbial Alexandria in Egypt. Kandahar in Afghanistan takes its own name too from the Macedonian conqueror, Alexander. The movement of Christianity to the West catalogued by historians has often overlooked much of this advance of Christianity in the East, usually excepting perhaps Constantinople. Granted, the persecution in Jerusalem did disperse the Christian population there, but many went eastward and not just westward because of it. To find an example of a very early Christian state and not one in Roman territory, we can look to Osrhoene, lying beyond the borders of the Roman Empire to the East. Its capital Edessa is better known, but not as well known is that the king there accepted Christianity for his people around the year 200, over a century before a Western emperor began his association with the Christian religion. Indeed, as some of the earliest Christians living on the edge of another empire, they sometimes found Persian administrators preferable to officials of the Roman Empire. All empires were not equal in terms of how they accommodated or treated Christians in their domains.

However, the notion of a universalism exuding from Christianity takes a while for the disciples to ingest, and particularly as Christianity was born within Judaism and with a Jew, Jesus. Nevertheless, Paul does seem to understand the message of Christ in its universal application and his strenuous journeys and successes and trials with that message have earned him the title of "Apostle to the Gentiles." In time, Gentile converts to the new faith will vastly outnumber Jewish converts to the Christian faith. The Jewish underpinnings of the Christian faith will therefore require a rather substantial and detailed explanation of what Christianity extracts from or owes to Judaism that might still be binding, but also what new light the new covenant in Christ sheds on the Jewish covenant and the Old Testament. Early on, the Christian community brings the Jewish Old Testament into its canon even as it is forming and selecting candidates for inclusion into its own New Testament canon. In Paul's letters in the New Testament, he will make notable contributions to the interface between the theology of the two testaments and the two faiths, for in many ways he is the most equipped to discuss the question. He had been an ardent and proud Jew, well-educated, and in days past, an active persecutor of the first generation of Christians. However, his famous "Damascus Road" conversion experience put him into the Christian camp, without leaving behind his ardent love and great respect for his own Jewish people. One might say that St. Paul never forgets his own even as he tries to bring them into an understanding of Christ.

CHRISTIAN INROADS INTO THE ROMAN WORLD

In significant contrast to the Jewish community, many and probably most of the early Christian converts, particularly if they were Gentiles, possessed few of the abilities of literacy, and this provoked many of the early critics of Christians to dub them ignorant followers of a predator religion. Moreover, given the religious desires that were mounting in Roman culture, it is hardly surprising that Christianity first established itself among the neediest. Hardening belief in the sufficiency of Rome and the empire to supply the needs of its population could easily produce a rebuke from not only the devoted and patriotic upper classes, but even from the slice of ordinary citizens who resented these religious supplicants offensively prostrate before their god instead of their emperor. With the strength of the empire on the wane, the presence of a new and "foreign" religion could serve as a painful and annoying reminder that the old Rome was under cultural siege. That is, streaming into the mix of all things Roman was a variety of peoples, philosophies, and religions, which were indicative of something of the cosmopolitan, but also increasingly chaotic nature of the place and times. Certainly the most visible to the discerning eye, even if sometimes shrouded in secrecy by adherents, were the mystery religions and their rituals. With justification, we might say that these religions evidenced adherents voraciously hungry for religious satisfactions that many outsiders looked upon with absolute abhorrence. The appeal of these religions to the upper classes and well-to-do was surely almost non-existent. The protectors of things Roman or things classical now had real reason to be—to exercise some discipline and critique of Rome going the way of all flesh. As earlier noted, Christianity endured this kind of critique in its first century of existence. Moreover, what one might call the pagan critique of the mystery religions and particularly Christianity was also complimented by a critique from some of these mystery religions of that mystery religion which appeared to be winning the day, though again almost exclusively among the ignorant masses—Christianity.

However, it was not only in the realm of the religious or spiritual that new winds were blowing in from the East, but new political conceptions were now playing their hand in some of the heads of the emperors, who clearly preferred to dress and mimic an oriental monarch. Alexander the Great centuries earlier had preferred this persona too, even as some within his ranks took offense at a conception smacking of despotism. So too, the receding of Rome as a republic only accentuated seeing the emperor in the role of extravagance if not to say deity. This conception, however, would produce an inevitable clash for Christians who prayed for the emperor without praying to him. Therefore, as the aftermath of the successes of Alexander's armies had brought the ways of the Greeks and Hellenism to the East, now some of the ways of the East were flowing in the reverse direction. The net effect was to produce something of a cosmopolitan culture with some churning. The eclectic atmosphere of the times would produce something of a reaction of the old against the new amongst some of the Roman nobility.

However, while the followers of the Christian religion in the beginning came from the lower classes, by the end of the second century, this religion had attracted some from virtually every level of society and every profession, and eventually, even governors of some Roman provinces showed some Christian sympathies. In some instances, however, the trains of conversions were precipitated by the devotion of a female family member who might impress a husband enough to bring him to the fold of the Christian community. Nevertheless, this dynamic was also criticized by the critic who faulted Christianity as revealing a feminine ethos.

Stoic philosophy, though born in the Hellenistic age, would promulgate itself into more and greater popularity during Roman times. The cosmopolitan emphasis of Stoicism is strong indication of its advocacy for a kind of universalism, for the Stoics would be adamant that they were not simply arguing for a local truth. Furthermore, if one lines up the most popular and influential of philosophies or intellectual ways of thinking arising out of the Hellenistic Age, Stoicism would be at or near the top. For something of the same reason, it was capable of being absorbed by or competing with to some degree the new religion that would overtake the Roman world eventually—Christianity.

Stoicism was perhaps the most elaborate and effective attempt of this period to try to mediate between the individual and the world in which he found himself. Ultimately, Stoicism encourages the kind of strength of character that can withstand adversities to the point that aspirants prove sufficient of themselves for mastery of the world they live in because they are masters of themselves. The Stoics, however, did not think the universe or reality as adversarial or alien to ourselves, but rather that the measure of reason and proportion that we find on exhibit in the world of nature can be captured in our own self-discipline. Such a realization would be sufficient to bring comfort to the aspiring Stoic that he is not a random thing in a random or irrational universe. The connection with reason is therefore important in Stoic aspiration and the goal of self-sufficiency, understood as something of an alignment with reason or logos or reality. This achievement exudes a kind of strength adequate for subduing travails.

For anyone familiar with the Christian ethic, it will be apparent how close but different such Stoic doctrines are compared to a Christian ethic. Moreover, to Stoics living in this period such as the Roman Emperor Marcus Aurelius (AD 121–180), the difference between the two conceptions could hardly be more distant or opposed to the other. This emperor openly expressed his view that the Christian ethic was one only viable for cowards and commoners, whom, he tended to think, most of humanity represents. At the same time, the Stoics, however, were also the first group of thinkers to call into question the common ancient proclivity for human slavery. This was an institution and cultural feature, for example, that neither Plato nor Aristotle had called into question.

JEWISH AND CHRISTIAN FUTURES

It is worthwhile to consider another aspect of the Jewish-Christian relationship. That is, given that the heritage of Christianity is wholly within Judaism, how had the cleft between the two become in effect so hardened by near the end of the first century? From the Christian perspective, the Jews had rejected their messiah, but their rejected messiah became the accepted messiah of the large Gentile Christian community. The Jewish rejection of

Jesus as the messiah, from the Christian perspective, was simply the latest in a long litany of rejection of various prophets of God by the Jewish people. From the Jewish perspective, Jesus was not the messiah because the messiah would come to usher in an age of peace and stability and oust the hated Romans, none of which this Jesus did. Indeed, the principle teachings of Jesus had clustered around his talking about the coming Kingdom of God, but from the Jewish perspective, no kingdom came. In other words, Pentecost brought no political changes. From the Christian perspective, however, this was to associate too closely the aims and purposes of Jesus with political and material goals of the Jews, rather than the ultimate purposes in the providence of God. These theological differences of Jesus and his message compared to Jewish expectations become so stark and then entrenched, that with the Council of Jamnia in AD 90, Jewish authorities codified their contention that one who was Jewish and who also accepted Jesus as the messiah, was by that coupling, no longer deemed a Jew. The net effect of such a ruling was to drastically demarcate Christian belief from Jewish belief and Christian from Jew.

Another reason prompting the meeting of the Council of Jamnia was that the Jewish community looked increasingly imperiled in terms of safety or even existence at the hands of the Romans. In AD 70, the Romans had destroyed the magnificent Temple in Jerusalem, after an uprising by the Jews against the Romans four years earlier that stretched on as the most strenuous revolt of the Jews against the Romans in Jewish history. After the temple was no more, the last element of remaining Jewish resistance tenaciously hung on, though quartered off on a mountain top named Masada, about a hundred miles from Jerusalem. The equally tenacious Romans built a ramp sufficient to get to the top of this virtually unreachable place, but found only dead Jews upon arrival, due to a mass suicide. Jerusalem soon became forbidden territory for Jews to enter, and the future of the Jews as a people seemed virtually without hope. When the Roman Empire finally collapsed in the centuries to come, the Jews would then find their most implacable foe in Christians. Here the old argument between them would be renewed and reinforced and very often repeated. That is, for many in the Christian camp, the Jews had not only rejected Jesus as messiah, but they had also killed him. Of course, the Romans had a very heavy hand of responsibility in the whole affair, but it was the Jews who were approving of the fate of Jesus. At the same time, the fate of the Jews in the deadly grip of the Romans elicited no noticeable Christian assistance for the Jews. This lack may have aided the Christians in the perception of Romans as an apolitical group, but also further removed if not nearly destroyed Jewish sympathies for Christians.

With the Old Testament canon being finalized at Jamnia by the Jewish community, the books that would become part of the Christian corpus or canon, were placed in another Testament, the New Testament. The Christian community would nevertheless incorporate the Old Testament into their Christian Bible, reaffirming Christian identity within Jewish history and expectations. At the same time, both believing communities now knew where they stand with reference to one another. However, severed from their homeland and in uneasy relationship with Christian communities, which in time became a Christian empire known as Christendom, the life and existence of Jews would often be precarious and dangerous. Moreover, though the Jews had excelled as a people, in their tendency to be clannish, they often drew a response not only of envy but suspicion.

CHRISTIAN EXPECTATIONS AND ORGANIZATION OF THE CHRISTIAN CHURCH

The apocalyptic nature of the Christian Gospel made a special appeal to many of the faithful and invigorated in them an expectation that the return of Christ would be imminent. The expectation naturally elicited optimism and some level of excitement. A study of the writings of St. Paul in the New

Testament, however, provides evidence that for many of the Christian community, Paul included, the expectation of what might be called the time table for Christ to come again would change from one of immediacy to one of patient anticipation. This look into the future, whether immediate or distant was of course not dissimilar to the prior Jewish expectation for a Messiah who would unwind them from the Roman yoke. For Christians, however, much of the Jewish expectation was colored by too many considerations pertaining to this world, that is, exchange of one regime for another. Early Christians had seen the powers of darkness bound, if not yet nullified by the coming of Christ, and the interim between the first and second coming would be a scenario in which a family or people or the like would be put in order, with neighbors told to expect the inevitable and certain judgment. The expectation of any real longevity attached to the interim period was scarcely present in the beginning.

Gradually, however, with successive Christian generations coming into being and dying, a need was prompted to plan for the future in a way that a community with an expectation of immediacy need not confront. At the same time, in beginnings of a more formal structure for the community of the Church, there was danger of lessened vigor and minimizing of the prophetic gifts that had been a central part of the Church in its earliest days. In the second and third century, a movement referred to as Montanism challenged the Church on most of these very points. One of the most important Latin fathers of the Church, Tertullian (c. AD 155–c. 240), eventually became an adherent of this sect, a sect that in earlier years he had severely criticized.

The Montanists would be regarded as obscurantists or primitivists or simply naïve by their more sophisticated critics because the organization of the Church by this time was increasingly governed by a hierarchy of officials whose offices ensured smoothness in times of transition, accountability, and procedures for dealing with doctrinal deviants and provided for supervision and discipline. Montanists, however, protested against the presumed benefits of such structures, which they generally deemed not only capable of suffocating the spiritual life out of Christians, but more importantly, they set the sights of Christians and their new masters on things of this world, rather than spiritual things. Therefore, the Montanists were advocates for intense spiritual discipline in expectation that the Parousia or second coming of Christ would indeed come as a thief in the night, as Christ had warned. The Montanists turned from officialdom and hierarchies to the spirited prophets found in their ranks, who dispensed the wisdom of God as men of God, not members of a calculating and strategizing Church now making itself akin to the establishment against which it had come into being by blood in the beginning. The Montanist's program was succinctly indicated in Tertullian's famous quip that "The blood of the martyrs is the seed of the Church." However, the morals of most Christians, in the estimations of the Montanists, were sorely lacking or at least tending toward the worldly.

While a generic form of Montanism would have a future in the history of the Church, principally, however, as the Christian prophetic spirit issued from some notable mystics and monks and itinerant preachers, underground house-churches, and fiery reformers and the like, it would have no future to speak of at this time. Because a structure for the Church was becoming slowly established and becoming useful to the necessary functions of an organization, to fall back on prophets and preachers for the future was for many a reversion to the checkered, uncertain, and bumpy past. In a simple comparison, it was the conflict between structure and spontaneity. Structure could provide some guarantees, while spontaneity could provide some needful illumination. To put the two in union without one squeezing the other out would not be an easy task in the history of the Christian Church.

Clarification might crush the spirit, but clarification was needed when the Church was beset by deviations from what it believed and taught and expected from its members. Theological clarifications for belief were soon enunciated and then established in the face of theological confusions which required some setting down of the boundaries of orthodox and unorthodox or heretical beliefs. If the Church was simply silent about such matters, the Church would suffer, but more importantly, suspected theological innovations and deviations required someone or a select body of people of the Church to address these problems and to make some firm and final decisions. Almost as important was the assigning of various people in the Church to care for various matters that Christian people should care for. These needs therefore required thought, planning, and execution. For this reason, people and structures had to be put into place to ensure success. The success of the prophet could be as spotty as his prophetic gift was spontaneous. On the other hand, the elimination of the exercise of the prophetic voice could commit the powers that be to listen only to themselves and thus spiritually stagnate or worse.

In the first century, the functionaries of the Church were really only two: the Apostle or preacher or Church planter and the congregation

The Ascending Christian Religion

planted and fed. The relationship was fairly intimate between the two, even as, in the case of St. Paul, the traveling missionary, his many Church plants necessitated that his time with individual congregations be spread over the many congregations. In his letters in the New Testament, the form of address to the congregation makes scarce mention of anyone except the congregation itself and presbyters and deacons. The larger role of bishop, moreover, would grow stronger and would start to assume the ultimate responsibility of spiritual care for a flock that had been assumed earlier largely by the presbyters. Even the bishop, however, was chosen in the earliest centuries in some manner by the congregants. However, as Christian numbers grew, indeed exploded in some places, the necessity for tighter structure began to place decision making at higher and higher levels. Negatively stated, the welcome news of higher counts of Christians ironically prompted the instigation of higher and broader levels of authority above the members of the congregation, who in time would find most decisions made above them and without them. Furthermore, upon reaching the fourth century, a hierarchy was established whereby it was necessary for the aspirant to have served in a number of capacities for a select period before advancement. With or without intention, the parallel with secular office or administrative position could reduce and tempt the occupant of position within this hierarchy to strain or compromise the spiritual component of his position. Not a few of the later medieval popes would acknowledge the difficulty of holding themselves up toward their spiritual responsibilities when awash in administrative matters.

Easily understood is the fact that the fastest growth of Christian numbers was in the cities, for in rural areas older religious habits and cultures tended to be more resistant to the changes coming with a new religion. The Christian federation that gradually developed eventuated in the predominance of the office of bishop and attached him to the cities, as the office sought to build and govern the Church in both places. Here, however, the generic problem of establishing rank or lines of authority at the highest level would become an issue. This particular issue provoked discussion, but not before the end of the fourth century did significant acrimony develop over an answer. At the same time, there scarcely had been a time when the Christian community and its leaders had not given deference and higher respect to some churches over others. Complicating the issue, however, was that to some significant degree, the weighty and respected Churches of Alexandria and Antioch—and Rome certainly—owed some and undoubtedly much of that respect to their secular and civic importance. Such would be much of the difficulty in trying to disentangle or demarcate secular and religious motivation or duty in the medieval centuries to come. However, beginning in the second century and escalating by a myriad of factors in the decades to come, lines of authority would be increasingly drawn to and from Rome. Even more, lines of authority would coalesce not only around the bishop of Rome or pope, but around the office of the emperor, especially when an emperor aligned himself with the Christian religion in the fourth century.

3

Formation of Medieval Civilization, 313–814

CHRISTIANITY AFTER CONSTANTINE

When Constantine made his affiliation with the Christian religion in 313, this ended one relationship of Christianity with the Roman Empire as another began. Before Constantine, some Roman emperors exhibited indifference, some toleration of this religion, while still others manifested moderate hostility and a few, severity. The Christian sect that grew from the theological ground of Judaism was by most accounts growing significantly in the various lands of the empire. Critics, however, deemed the expanding number of adherents and some Christian ideas detrimental to Roman culture and civilization. Some of the most vocal critics were political leaders.

To posterity, Nero (AD 37–68) is the most notorious of opponents of the Christians, particularly notable for his part in the deaths of Peter and Paul and for sometimes setting Christian bodies ablaze as night torches for the imperial city. Whereas Nero sent some of the sect called Christians to suffer combat with wild animals in the famous Coliseum, Constantine banned this kind of grotesqueness in that arena. Constantine, however, was far from unblemished in his own rule or life. Political life in the empire as it extended into the medieval period of Western history would remain generally violent. More importantly, after Constantine, persecution of the Church faded. The new and different circumstances for Christians would eventually, in part, prompt the rise of the influential monastic orders.

The previous threat and reality of martyrdom served to keep the Church from lackadaisical or lascivious living in an empire sometimes uneasy with or hostile to Christians. However, with an emperor now Christian overseeing the empire and lending the occasional and protective hand to the Church, Christians could unwittingly slip into habits of a leisured, because safe, group. The seriousness of the monastic life therefore provided a way of giving one's all to God in living devotion after the deadly martyrdom of the past subsided.

The earliest ventures toward monasticism were undertaken by some brave or even odd and cantankerous individuals preferring the remoteness of solitary life for drawing near to God. Other and more sociable types opted for life in a communal monastery. Here monastic communities lived, worked, and worshipped together. The monastic life invigorated these followers of Christ through a disciplined regimen and produced in time not a few notable leaders of the Church. The penchant for monasticism, however, before it became a staple of medieval civilization, troubled some leaders of the Church. They initially expressed hesitations about this kind of spiritual life.

Eventually, however, some monks became notable and inspiring popes; Gregory the Great (590–604) would be the first. Gregory was also probably the first Bishop of Rome to accept that the Christian Church was burgeoning with new but raw converts lacking virtually any of the accoutrements or vestiges of past Roman culture. The people who had been invaders of the Roman Empire were now occupants of a world that would be fashioned differently because they were distinctly different. These different people some Romans contemptuously referred to as "barbarians," though hardly Gregory. There were many bands or tribes among them, but all Germanic in origin, with the exception of the dreaded Huns, probably from Mongolia. Even the feared Germanic tribes trembled before these warriors as much as the nervous and calculating Romans. In the centuries of a collapsing empire, the Romans and barbarians would sometimes bind together against the formidable Huns. On other occasions, the Huns might unite with other tribes of barbarians against the Romans. Scarcely any tribe or coalition of tribes felt safe for very long from their adversaries. The eastern part of the empire would not suffer as much devastation and disruption from the barbarian invasions as the western lands. There was a relative safety found in the East and in Constantinople compared to the devastation in the western regions of the empire. Still, Rome carried the name of the land masses of the empire, even in Constantinople.

Gregory's background was that of a prominent Roman family. Many and probably most Roman families significantly resented the uncouth and unlearned barbarian intruders whereas Gregory made a strenuous attempt to assimilate them to the Christian faith and Church. Meanwhile, they were illiterate in nearly total numbers; Gregory had a mountain of work before him and his successors. The example and situation would be testament to the fact that civilization, from about Gregory's time, would be virtually contiguous with the Christian religion and the Church and the monastic orders.

Noting some collapsing moments for the old empire between Constantine and Gregory enables one to see that what Constantine did in 313 did not spare the weakening empire from the tumult of encroachment by the tribes. They continued to overrun and infiltrate the shell of the once mighty empire. For his part, Constantine surely evaluated the assets in the leaders and structures of the Church for purposes of hope for the dying empire. However, he was not simply or only an opportunist seeking to save one institution for the price of another. Nonetheless, his affiliation and comportment with Christianity swirls with debate. Like most significant leaders, actions are probably the best key to understanding motivations. Some observers, for example, count Constantine sincere but superstitious for requiring his soldiers to paint the Christian cross on their shields before battle. Others count him more a politician than anything else. In 325, Constantine called the important Council of Nicaea in the East to settle a theological dispute. Constantine, however, seemed more interested in the stability of his empire than in the real solidity or satisfaction of any solution purporting to settle a theological matter. Nevertheless, his motivations are perhaps as much as one might expect from a man who served his countrymen not only as a devotee of Christ but also as their Caesar.

Constantine's father, also a Roman emperor (Constantius Chlorus), had exhibited some sympathy to Christianity. His attitude, just like those with less or no sympathy, indicates that this religion had too much public presence to be ignored by officials. There were, therefore, decisions and divisions among the old Romans over the two newcomers: barbarians and Christians. Undoubtedly, many Romans felt more affinity for the old Rome than the one being reconfigured in another image. Particularly galling to some was the social status of many converts attracted to Christianity, including women, the poor, and the outcasts. This judgment would of course include hordes of barbarians. Constantine's mother, Helena, nevertheless, was a seriously devout person of the Christian faith. Indeed, she may have been more pious than her famous emperor son. Eventually converts would begin to come from the upper tiers of Roman society, and from there, some Christian intellectuals addressed the offense taken by some Romans over Christian converts. These new apologists for the Christian faith contended that the Christian God was not a respecter of the station in life of anyone. This belief would have addled some Romans, but attracted others. The notion of equality, even equality before God, was probably most putrid to many living in the upper classes of Roman society, even as some from the upper classes joined the new religion.

Stories such as the troubling but provocative Gospel account of Pilate's wife coming to the Roman governor during the trial of Jesus were portends for the Gospel making inroads anywhere and everywhere, to the most unlikely of peoples. Interestingly enough, just as women had some prominence in the life of Jesus as portrayed in the Gospels, so too we observe something of that inclusion in this time period. Indeed, that Pilate's wife was troubled about the man on trial would anticipate the tradition that she became a follower of the accused whose death her husband had supervised. Furthermore, when the chieftain of the first of the many Germanic tribes submitted to the Church for baptism, Clovis of the Franks around 496—and 3000 of his Frankish warriors on the same day—it was probably because of his wife, Clotilde, who had been a Christian for some years before. The women in the Gospel stories are thus not the last time we hear about prominent females in the history of the followers of Christ. Of course, such cultural associations as these were hardly assets to many Romans who often snubbed Christians. The Romans were a proud people and especially proud of a heritage they wanted to protect from forces seeming to turn it in another and more dubious direction. The Christians held up a man who had been crucified; some Roman citizens, by contrast, honored their rulers as near deities and strong men who from strength put weaker men on crosses. Diocletian, an emperor some few years before Constantine, openly presented himself with an aura of the divine; as a result, he was an active opponent of the Christian population who worshipped their own God-Man, Christ.

Constantine's later association with the Christian religion therefore drew a significant amount of criticism that continued after him. His nephew, named Julian the Apostate (360–363), thought his uncle had plunged Roman culture in a downward direction by extending imperial favor to this foreign and rather revolting religion, but by Julian's time, the train was too far out of the station. Julian could not turn the clock or the culture back.

When Constantine wanted to remake the city of Rome into a new Christian Rome, opposition proved too strong, so he built his Christian city in Constantinople, further to the East. After all, this was the region where the Christian religion had come from in the beginning. Indeed, while Peter and other Christian worthies had met their end in Rome, the initial believers came out of Jerusalem in the East. The East would be theologically astute too, plus aesthetically enticing, assets their brethren in the West found difficult to match, particularly given the calamities from tribes pushing into their frontiers and finally into their most splendid of cities, Rome itself.

CHRISTIANITY AFTER THE ROMAN EMPIRE

The advance of newcomers and converts and the eventual collapse of the fabric of the old Western Roman Empire meant that in time, non-Romans would be in charge of the world that they had collapsed. These Germanic infiltrators lacked almost everything the sophisticated Roman world possessed except military might. That barbarian military strength had trounced some Roman legions at the Battle of Adrianople in 378. The barbarians had in fact killed an Eastern Roman Emperor who commanded the defeated. Hearing of this disastrous first defeat of a Roman army at the hands of the barbarians sent chills down the Roman spine.

The barbarians for their part needed and enviously respected Romans for the latter's abilities to orchestrate and manage an empire. The Romans, for their part, had earlier needed and used some barbarian soldiers not fighting against them to fill out the vast but dwindling Roman armies fighting other Germans or Huns. By this route, some of the barbarian chieftains worked themselves eventually into high and powerful positions as generals. From here the final toppling of the old Rome would only be a matter of finite time. Eventually, a powerful Germanic tribal chieftain named Odoacer deposed the to-be, but not to-be Emperor Romulus in 476. The chieftain Odoacer therefore took the emperor's position, meant for a Roman, from a Roman. Now the barbarians were not only winning in the field and the lands of the Romans, but also in the contest for political power over the Romans.

Constantinople, however, only grudgingly referred to Odoacer, and certainly not as any emperor, but merely as a king. Many historians date this specific event of political spiral downward as the symbolic end of a very long chapter of Western and Roman history. The Christian Roman Empire would now be understood or gauged as politically headquartered in Constantinople, even as the Bishop of the city of Rome continued to acquire more power and prestige as the spiritual head of Christendom.

Earlier yet and painfully endured too was the partial sacking of the eternal city of Rome in 410 by the Visigoth chieftain Alaric. For Romans and those of Roman sympathies, to include of course most Christians at this time period, this physical event, laden with significant material destruction, was cataclysmic for the population. Hardly anything worse was conceivable to those enduring this disaster, for some Christians had thought the empire and the faith could be one. Others like St. Augustine (353–429), the Christian thinker, thought the association of the Church and the world dubious.

With the calamity of the fall of the old empire, the growing Christian world could scarcely manage effective control of what was left, despite the expenditure of impressive work and energy. Some of the old Romans took up the chant that their world died because Romans had not been vigilant in paying homage to the Roman protector gods. Indeed, as some of the Roman emperors evoked an air of deity about them and expected a corresponding adulation, this expectation was a liability that the early Christian community sometimes fell afoul of to the point of death. Thus, it was not just the burgeoning Christian numbers that were galling to some, but again, various Christian ideas were deemed ruinous to the point of traitorous to the Roman state and culture. However, on the larger point—that the old world was eclipsing because of the introduction of the new Christian deity—the Christian community found a ready respondent in Augustine of North Africa.

Augustine and Thomas Aquinas of the thirteenth century are on most reckonings esteemed as the most gifted and influential minds of the Middle Ages. The story of Augustine before he became of such stature is illustrative of a turbulent life as well as the tumultuous times of his day. Though he had a Christian mother, his father was pagan. Augustine himself as a youth exasperated his mother with his rejection of his mother's religion. He moved intellectually through multiple phases of varying beliefs, philosophical and religious, sprinkled with a voracious sensual appetite that kept him at bay from the Christian religion even as he eventually began to be drawn back toward it. In Augustine's later *Confessions*, he recounts the story of a moral conversion that sent him to his mother's Church as the eventual Archbishop of Hippo.

Along the route of his return to Christianity, Augustine made some new friends from the Roman and Greek past, particularly Cicero, Plotinus, but most of all Plato. He regarded the thoughts of these prior thinkers as stepping stones for him and others to the truth of Christianity. Nevertheless, Augustine was not an intellectual's intellectual, for he proposed the purpose of knowledge to be for human salvation. Knowledge was not simply for the sake of knowledge itself, as the Greek thinker Aristotle had thought. Thus, though Augustine takes up many of the familiar topics and themes of other thinkers and philosophers, his thought, even on the subject of time, which we also find in his *Confessions*, is brought back to God.

The grace of God that spared the wandering and wayward early life of Augustine would commit him to take significant issue with a British monk named Pelagius (c. 360–c. 420). Augustine thought that Pelagius scarcely acknowledged the requirement of the grace of God for human salvation. In this way, Augustine was reminiscent of St. Paul, who had argued against the "Judaizers" of his day as relying upon themselves rather than the grace of God in Christ. Pelagius simply sped too quickly to the notion of a human sufficiency that erased the need for God's grace. In time too, Augustine would pen the first Christian philosophy of history in his *City of God*. In this work he took aim at the pagan contention that the empire was suffering because the Christian God had replaced neglected and now vengeful Roman gods.

Meanwhile the frail and now failing human city crumbled as Augustine's own city of Hippo lay under siege by the tribe of the Vandals as he lay dying. The old Roman civilization was imploding. Some of the residual Roman community might find service in the rule of the newly resident tribal peoples. Boethius (c. 480–526) belonged to an old Roman family, but also embraced the Christian family. In the century after Augustine he would find his niche in administration while he translated some of the works of

Plato and Aristotle. Historians debate whether Boethius or his predecessor Augustine should be counted the last thinker of the classical age, because they were essentially of Roman cultural heritage, but existentially fraught with the transitions to another culture and world. Boethius found work in the service of Theodoric the Ostrogoth (475–526), the chieftain who then controlled vast territories of former Roman real estate. This man managed to persuade the emperor at Constantinople to give him the title of viceroy of the eastern portion of the empire. When the Emperor Zeno at Constantinople persuaded him to go to war with the forces of Odoacer, Theodoric obliged him and capped his victory off by killing Odoacer himself at a banquet celebrating Theodoric's victory.

Theodoric, however, imprisoned and ultimately had Boethius killed as traitorous, indicative probably of the continued subtle but seething hostility between the Romans and their replacements. The relationship between the two was almost always uneasy and probably no better reflected than in the statement circulated at the time that while no Roman desired to be a Goth, every Goth desired to be a Roman. The tribes were now in charge of their betters. Resentments were probably in no short supply from either adversary.

Resenting, but probably not fearing the occupying tribes enough, the most notable emperor at Constantinople for all time, named Justinian (527–565), decided that the old empire needed restoration. That is, as much as Constantine had wanted a Christian empire, so did Justinian. Moreover, like some prominent men of his day, he was not of Rome lineage, but he was schooled in the shadow of the great empire. He had been born in the far afield Balkans, in the possession of Macedonia at the time, to Latin-speaking parents and brought to Constantinople by his uncle. Soon after he assumed the throne, Justinian prepared to take back from the uncouth barbarians virtually all the land the barbarian tribes had confiscated. This project notably started from the eastern side of Christendom. The East had managed to keep more grandeur, wealth, and other resources from the ruin that had dropped the West into the hands of the barbarians.

Meanwhile, however, Justinian set about his hopeful work of restoration, but he hugely drained the resources of the East to remake the West. While largely successful in his initial military operations, Justinian's gains of territory could not be maintained, and the end result was hardly worth the huge expenditures undertaken for such a colossal task. Most historians have judged him harshly for a major miscalculation. Despite such a catastrophe, however, his feats, such as the building of the monumental and magnificent Hagia Sophia in a mere six years and the compilation of the law code that goes by his name, are truly remarkable.

EAST AND WEST

The East and the West had different though related histories as the ushering in of the medieval period of Western history began. The two were joined under a single but frequently not a unified religion. An emperor in Constantinople stood in uneasy alliance with one powerful Bishop of Rome. The overwhelming distance encompassed from east to west was sufficient in itself for little more than a less than firm relationship between the two frontiers of Christendom. However, there was more to put if not enmity between them, at least envy. That is, the Eastern empire had the earliest Christian communities, among them some of the Pauline, and even more revered, the very ground that Jesus had trod upon. Possession of this geography alone was perhaps sufficient to enable the Eastern Christian community to see itself as birthing the original Christian story and first communities of Christian faith. Indeed, of the five patriarchal cities, the East had four—Constantinople, Alexandria, Antioch, and Jerusalem; the West had one—Rome.

The East too had the earliest theologians, and later Easterners retained a firm grasp of the Greek language, something lost for the most part in the West in a relatively brief time. The East, however, would have its own theological controversies to deal with, just as Augustine had to deal with Pelagianism. Nevertheless, the theological and political base of the East seemed firmer than that of the West. Regarding the former, there was a rich theological tradition referred to as the Church Fathers that largely came from the Eastern Church and was tremendously respected by Christian thinkers of later centuries. Indeed, the writings of these Church Fathers were historically prized by their Western counterparts. However, partly due to the disruptions occurring in the West, after the time of Gregory the Great, almost none of the Western clergy could read these writings in the original tongue of Greek. There is notable exception to this lack in the case of Irish monasticism, where Greek remained familiar. This was in great part because churchmen in Ireland were isolated enough to avoid some of the catastrophes besetting their weakened Western neighbors to the east.

The Roman bishop assumed greater and greater prestige among the various congregations and patriarchal cities. Constantinople and the East, feeling themselves the closest to the Christian faith both geographically and historically and linguistically and with stronger theological edifices, came to be in an ever uneasy relationship with the Western Church through the medieval period. We might say the East saw itself as originating earlier and therefore, as purer than the West, while the latter saw itself as oriented toward the needful and the practical. However, there was one exception to the East seeming to best the West in that the East had given rise to some significant deviations from the orthodox Christian faith, whereas Rome itself appeared to be relatively unspotted by comparison. It was also and forever the place of martyrdom of Peter and Paul.

The thinkers and leaders of the East were more mystically inclined than those of the West, and a comparison of the monastic traditions of each exhibits a contrast due to different conceptions of living the Christian life as a monk. That is, the monks of the East were meditative and contemplative types which produced and inculcated in their habits the mystical approach to the monastic Christian life. Here monks gave their whole duty and attention to God. To eat and acquire other requirements of maintaining life and existence, they turned to the lay community who supplied these necessities for the support required for one giving his all to God.

Beginning with the Western Benedictine order first installed at Monte Casino, Italy, by St. Benedict in 529, manual work became something of a standard part of the Western monastic life. This almost necessarily put such orders in closer association with the world outside the monastery. The social impetus in such orders therefore contributed to monastic traditions which in time might and did gravitate toward the world, while the Eastern monastic traditions vied hard to keep themselves unspotted from the world. The Eastern monks therefore tended to be more reclusive while Western monks for the most part tended to be industrious, sometimes both for the Gospel and for gain. Because of the energy of some of the monastic Western traditions, wealth was an issue they oftentimes had to face, whereas their monastic brethren of the East rarely had the mechanisms in place to inherit that problem.

The ascendancy of Gregory the Great to the papacy, though a relatively short rule of about fourteen years, gave direction to the Church at Rome and the Catholic tradition unrivaled by most other popes. Though contemplative by temperament, he was also a master of organization. Such a gift was imperative because the old Rome and its supporting structures were in shambles. Someone was needed who could plug the holes left by the disappearance of much of the old Roman fabric. Religiously, however, his accomplishments were no less great and in them, moreover, he showed perhaps his greatest skill at organization. When his attention was drawn to the state of the far island of England, he enlisted a monk named Augustine from Gregory's own monastic background to initiate the Roman mission among the English. Insistent upon the necessity and virtue of obedience for the work of men doing the work of God, Gregory also set in motion the requirement of appointed archbishops first journeying to the pope at Rome for their installation. Initiating this schemata first in England, it would continue with later popes. Meanwhile, Gregory would instruct his initiate Augustine to go first to southeastern England, for in the domain of Kent, the ruler was married to a Christian princess from the tribe of the Franks.

Apparently indefatigable, this Benedictine pope also managed to write a biography on the founder of the Benedictines, St. Benedict. He knew the Eastern half of Christendom well, because he spent almost six years as a Roman papal envoy at Constantinople. The pope who sent Gregory would be succeeded by Gregory as pope—probably a testament to the elder man's awareness of the younger man's gifts. While at Constantinople, he had been given the mission of convincing his Eastern brethren to lend a protecting hand against the barbarian Lombard assaults on Rome and Italy. This effort came to naught, however, and probably provided Gregory with the realization that the West would have to fend for itself. This would be difficult, and as further example of it, he had to shift the London headquarters from London to Canterbury because the pagan Saxon presence was still too strong at London. Indeed, any restoration of the old "Pax Romana" was scarcely yet possible; in 581, the first Benedictine monastery at Monte Casino was sacked by the Lombards. Soon, moreover, the West, and indeed the East too, would have yet another invader at its doors. In 884 Monte Casino was sacked yet again and then destroyed by the newcomers, called the Saracens. This was a name commonly used by medieval people in referencing Muslims.

THE RISE OF ISLAM

Mohammed died in 632, a couple of decades after the death of Gregory. The later years of Mohammed's life gave notice and warning to the surrounding peoples that a new force was rising in the world. During these years, the conquest of most all the Arabian peninsula had been accomplished and a mere hundred years after Mohammed's death, sizable portions of Europe, India, China and most of today's Middle East were within the Islamic Empire. However, this new empire was not just a political entity enveloping lands and territory, but a religious body claiming contentious heritage with the Jewish and Christian faiths. Moreover, Islam was insistent to supersede them with its message of the *Koran* and Allah's final messenger, Mohammed. This would place the East and West of Christendom in uneasy relationships with a new neighbor and sometimes in spasmodic conflict with Islam.

Though Jews and Christians were often referred to in the *Koran* and by Islamists as "People of the Book," the elevation of the *Koran* by Muslims over the Jewish Old Testament and the Christian New Testament presented serious theological differences with Jews and Christians that seemed intractable. The *Koran* and Islam were taken by adherents of this newest and youngest of the Semitic religions as superseding and correcting the earlier but corrupted Jewish and Christian scriptures. Pointing at Christianity especially, Islam took exception to the Christian claim about the deity of Christ and so too the Christian doctrine of the Godhead, or Trinity. In one manner of speaking, Islam saw itself as a simple but sufficient religion, such that in time those on the outside of this new faith would capitulate to the logic of Islamic theology and willingly subscribe to it as the true religion. This kind of passive optimism may help account for the relative tolerance Islam sometimes had for other faiths found under its political umbrellas.

Meanwhile those Christians living under Islamic jurisdictions found themselves paying more in taxes than their Islamic neighbors. However, political leaders, glad for the extra tax, could evidence hesitancy toward religious conversions which garnered less tax monies from the infidel after his conversion. This religious and political bifurcation sometimes evident in Islam, though certainly similar to tensions in Christianity between the imperial and the religious centers of that civilization, nevertheless seemed muted in Islam in other periods of its history. That is, in its first hundred years, Islam made substantial, indeed seismic, gains geographically. Even though the earlier growth of Christianity was certainly impressive in the beginning, Christianity was nevertheless outweighed by the beginning Islamic meteoric geographical advances in the world. This massive growth was in part because Christian culture came later to joining the things of

God to the things of Caesar. In other words, however weakly implied the doctrine of the division and separateness of state and the church was in Western thought, Islamic culture tended to fuse what Western Christian culture sometimes held uneasily together in the medieval period, or in modernity, could rip asunder. The future model of a secular state can be anticipated from the history of medieval Christian civilization, but is less conceivable from the history of medieval Islamic civilization.

Therefore, the political dimension of Islam was the primary point of contact for Christian civilization with Islam in the beginning. Indeed, it sometimes appears that it was the political successes of Islam that prompted theological attention from Christian quarters. This could occur in circuitous ways. One example is the Iconoclastic Controversy in the Eastern Church, which came on the heels of Islamic expansive gains of territory. Eastern churchmen might have had occasion to ask themselves if there was any correlation between the two. That is, were the rapid successes of the Islamic advance perhaps due to Moslem obedience to the prohibition against images in Islamic law? Suddenly, therefore, the Eastern sector of Christianity, which had been awash in icons and pictures and visual feasts for much of its history, began to question if these means of devotion were even appropriate for worship of the true and one God.

In the Islamic capture of areas of the East like Syria, Islam became heir to much of the classical Greek heritage preserved in such places. In time, this would permit Islamic scholars, translating the Greek into Arabic for themselves, to be in possession of a literary inheritance largely lost to Western culture. It was almost a half a millennium before the West would become aware that Islamic culture had such a stash. To know that, however, they need not have gone to Syria or to the East for that matter, for Islam was in Western Europe's southern portal in Iberia by 712.

Historians have gauged that part of the rapid growth of Islam a hundred years after Mohammed's death occurred by managing to capitalize on susceptibilities besetting Christian civilization at this time. Because of the rift of some groups of Eastern Christians who had to endure some severe accountability to Constantinople, some groups seemed to have welcomed a new regime that treated them with more leniency than their Eastern, though Christian masters. The Egyptian Church, to be known as the Copts, was in this category. Encountering weak resistance in such regions as Egypt, the Islamic advance continued around the Mediterranean until it crossed into Iberia from North Africa. Here the Visigoth culture was militarily unprepared for such an adversary, and the Islamic force pushed Christian Visigothic culture back and up into the northern edges of Iberia. Though sometimes pockets of resistors came out to harass and occasionally best their conquerors, it was not until the Reconquista in the thirteenth century that Iberia would retake Iberia back for itself. By then, however, the number of converts to Islam was a sizable portion of the population. The re-Christianization of Iberia would not be a swift process.

When Western scholars started to discover the treasure trove of Classical writings that were in the hands of Islamic scholars, some of the first steps toward the high Middle Ages were planted. This is why, moreover, the most adept Western scholars at that later time were those very few who could read Arabic. This is the reason the scholar most sought was the translator—for those many not knowing Arabic. Now laborious work would be undertaken to get behind the Arabic translation of the Greek so as to get the Greek into Latin for Western scholars. Even by the time of the high Middle Ages, few Westerners had yet mastered Greek. Most of those who did came from Ireland.

ESTABLISHING THE ROMAN CHURCH

The origins of Christianity and Christian learning in Ireland are obscure. Some have speculated that perhaps Greek speakers from the eastern Mediterranean settled in this island nation. Whatever the case, the Irish and Celtic culture the settlers produced lacked import from the Roman Church. Unsurprisingly, therefore, the liturgical year and times of religious festivals were different, and Irish churchmen did not organize their Church in the pattern of dioceses as did Rome. Perhaps most notably, the leaders of this Church were the abbots of monasteries, themselves given to sophisticated theological study. The monastic schools produced an educated clergy second to none in Western Europe at the time.

Moreover, Gregory the Great became aware of this distant Christian enclave that was not Roman in organization and he feared perhaps not amendable to assimilation. However, Gregory felt the need to incorporate this obviously gifted Christian people into the Church of Christ at Rome. Resistance on the part of the Irish stalled that endeavor for some time and, coupled with the later and savage Scandinavian onslaught into Irish monasteries, precipitated an eventual Irish decline. However, the missionary activity of the learned Irish in the interim injected itself into the changing landscape of neighboring northern England, where the Germanic Angles and the Saxons were being slowly assimilated into the Christian Church. One might say then that the impetus of the Irish passed partly to the converted Angles and Saxons, who took the Christian message back to the continent. The residue of Irish work persisted, however. After Charlemagne began his school at Aachen, later school officials managed to cajole the greatest thinker of the ninth century, John Scotus Erigena of Ireland, to come to this school.

Significantly, lest we forget the rustic nature of the Germanic tribes, even some of their leaders before the turn of the millennium were still barely literate. The cultured sophistication of the old Roman Empire was gone, but would get a new boost from the work of the most famous king of the Franks, named Charlemagne (768–814).

The ever perceptive Pope Gregory the Great, almost two centuries before Pope Leo III crowned Charlemagne in St. Peter's, surmised that this group of newcomers, the Franks, were potential partners with the struggling Roman Church of Gregory's day. Gregory's hope seems not to bring a state into the service of the Church, but rather to reckon with a kingdom of this world at least somewhat favorable toward the goals of the Church. Gregory had written letters to the Merovingian successors of Clovis, but to no avail. Clovis himself was the first Frankish leader to submit himself to the Christian rite of baptism, though his life seemed little different after taking the religion of his Christian wife. Nevertheless, when Clovis's Merovingians had the purple wrested from them by the Carolingians, Pope Gregory's successors found these rulers of the Franks more hospitable toward the Church. Some of the strongest evidence of this attitude to the Church was the readiness of the Carolingians to look favorably upon the work of Anglo-Saxon Christian missionaries from England in rough and tumultuous Gaul. One of these missionaries in particular, a Benedictine named Winifred, his name Latinized to St. Boniface, traversed incredible distances and domains within the lands of the Franks and Germans.

The Carolingian ruler during much of this time was Charles Martel, grandfather of the eventual Charlemagne. Martel was cautious but accepting toward the efforts of the Church in his domains, and something only short of an alliance developed in the relationship between the two. Charles Martel must have been extraordinarily impressive to the Roman clergy and missionaries, for it was he in 732 at Poitiers (or Tours) who finally stopped any further advance of Islamic armies into Frankish territory. In Western history books, this feat is counted one of the most significant in that it made or kept Western Christian civilization relatively intact and preserved it, for some future time, from further ravages. In Islamic history, this event is oftentimes omitted, but not quite for the reason one might suspect—possibly embarrassment. Rather, from the perspective of Islam, its armies sought the much greater prize in the grander culture and wealth of Byzantium—Constantinople. The defeat at Tours was not much loss, because a victory there would have hardly been a win. Constantinople, by contrast, would have been a trophy. Nevertheless, it was the Franks who were deemed in charge of the Western empire by the Moslems. Even at the time of the later Crusades, still almost a half millennium away, Islam continued to speak of the Crusaders as the Franks.

An alliance between the Franks and the papacy found firmer ground in Gaul as time went on, and even the rulers of the Carolingians might take to the monastery themselves, as did one of the sons of Charles Martel, who, in 747, went to be a monk at Monte Casino. The family did for the most part see in relationship with the papacy benefit to their kingdom and the papacy was hopeful that Frankish leaders might produce a leader capable of restoring the place for an emperor in the West. Around the same time, the papacy was distressed to learn that the Emperor in the East was expecting the Roman Church to obey its iconoclastic decrees. The West dissented. From the perspective of the Church in Rome, the Emperor in the East had no such religious authority as he assumed, for religious authority issued from the Bishop of Rome. Even Gregory the Great had sanctioned the use of visual messengers in his famous contention that "Images are the books of the unlearned." Certainly the East had a greater literacy than its Western brothers, and thus the deficient West could more easily appreciate the applicability of Gregory's justification in their situation.

It is hardly surprising then that those in the East tended to see themselves as above the rather rustic and ruffian West. However, another worry soon emerged. The crowning of Charlemagne on Christmas Day in 800 by the pope was not impressive to Eastern observers, but rather cause for alarm. Indeed, this was an act laden with the real possibility of schism between the Eastern and Western Church. Furthermore, this was an act of usurping the one emperor in Constantinople. Constantinople would hereafter refer to Charlemagne as a king, but not as an emperor. The divide and disgruntlement of East with West and West with East was hardening.

Charlemagne proved to be a dutiful son of the Church, but his crowning by the Roman head of the Church in 800 probably did not indicate to him any subservience to the pope. Indeed, when Charlemagne's chosen successor son, called Louis the Pious, was crowned almost a half century later, the story goes that Charlemagne explicitly did not extend an invitation to the pope. As such tensions suggest, cobbling together political and religious authority in the Western medieval world would prove difficult Even when emperors were Christian in more than name and popes approached everything they were expected to be, conflicts were still common. Some conflicts subdued emperors or kings and sometimes popes and sometimes both. Such conflicts were sometimes most hurtful to the ordinary person of the Middle Ages.

4

Fruits of the Burgeoning Medieval Civilization, 814–1054

CHARLEMAGNE

Charlemagne had two daughters who became nuns, though hardly of their own will. Some nobles provided sons or daughters to a monastery or convent, thereby solidifying further the conjunction of political and religious authority during the medieval period. However, as new political threats emerged from outside the nexus of the Church and Western Europe, what stability Charlemagne and the papacy had given to Europe would seem in peril yet again as the Norsemen made their way south. The relative peace that Charlemagne had brought for a time would now suffer major disruption. His sons and grandsons proved not to be his equal in governing.

Charlemagne's political successes are largely attributable to his military might, while his responsibility for some new learning in the form of what would later be termed by historians as the "Carolingian Renaissance," issues from a man, unlearned himself and scarcely literate, who saw the need for something sorely lacking in his domains and officials. His school, located at present day Aachen, Germany, and on the French border, was a place where scholars of particular note in his day and after were invited, and where the scriptorium made copies of most of the classical documents they possessed and we would not possess today, but for the labors of these and other copyists.

Probably most troubling to Charlemagne was the lack of learning in his domains and his exposure to how astoundingly ill-equipped were the vast majority of parish priests only weakly instructing the faithful, because they lacked even basic skills of learning. The vast majority of them were illiterate themselves. The common people were even more so. This lack is one that we can hardly understand the medieval world without, if we are to comprehend how life must have been for medieval people.

Years before Charlemagne died in 814, the advances of the Norsemen were already afflicting Europe. The scourges from the tribes that constituted this new group of marauders surely equaled the terror felt by Europeans facing the Huns centuries earlier. The Huns were versatile and sleek warriors on horseback, whereas the quickness of the strikes of the Vikings came from swift and small boats. Moreover, the boats became larger and more. The booty that initial Viking raids carried off surely conveyed to these warriors the immensity of the riches ripe for their piracy.

These warriors naturally tended to strike at places where resources were large and defenses meager or none. This calculation necessarily drew the marauders to places like monasteries. As these tended to be places where learning and study were undertaken too, the loss from the strikes of Norsemen warriors upset these islands of clinging civilization hardest. Furthermore, due to the proximity of island geography to Viking sea lanes, the British Isles and the northern parts of France suffered immensely. The situation was especially dour considering the precarious cultural impetus earlier launched by Charlemagne. If this king seemed to have turned the course of the dark ages before him into a Renaissance after him that bears his name, the Viking exploits seemed capable of upending any advances, however small, and now seemingly precarious.

The Norsemen coming out of the north, coupled with Saracen and Hungarian raids, would have overloaded any leaders of the day. Interestingly, the successors of Charlemagne were more men of the Church than they were strong political rulers. Coupling these two reasons together with others, we begin a period of fragmentary feudalism in which people and communities sought safety from danger in places where they could find it. A fragmented and decentralized society sought for solace in places where the needed protection favored the rise of lords offering such protection. To varying degrees, the people living under such protection reciprocated their need for safety by serving their lord. This kind of relationship becomes the common social and political institution in a world in seeming dissolution and lacking a unified and centralized base of power, such as that found in a later strong nation king. Not all of Europe evolved into this kind of feudal society at the same time or same rate. However, more importantly, this

Fruits of the Burgeoning Medieval Civilization

stratification of power was prompted generally by weak leadership dwarfed by distance and too little care for the needs of people seeking security. In a society breaking into pieces and with frequent violence, populations naturally felt vulnerable. In time some of the lords grow powerful enough to win the prestige of collecting taxes and conducting judicial courts. By gaining this kind of control, some lords and vassals eventually gain enormous and competing power. The more powerful vassals and nobles would become dukes, and their power was such that they not infrequently managed to have armies even larger than their aspiring kings.

AFTER THE CAROLINGIANS

The Carolingian family eventually lost their royal crown in 987. They had managed no real control over their presumed subsidiary leaders or dukes for many prior generations. The title of king west of the Rhine River would now go to the powerful lord, Hugh Capet (987–996). However, the lord now king would encounter similar problems with his dukes, and in great part, because many of the previous assailants, namely Vikings, took up occupancy in the lands of Hugh. Eventually, he realizes that they are hardly his lands anymore because of the amassing of power by the newcomers. This new duchy of Normandy by 1040 falls under the grip of the power of the infamous William, who soon starts to turn his eyes toward what lay across the English Channel. In 1066, he makes his move and is known to history as William the Conqueror.

The work of Charlemagne and Alcuin, his hand-picked man for advancing education, however, was not lost by what came after the Carolingians. Particularly in the eastern provinces of the Frankish inheritance, where the Viking intrusions disrupted the least, learning was preserved and slowly advanced again. Moreover, the desire to recoup as much as possible of the classical traditions and the writings of the Church Fathers continued. However, the conditions were not yet in place for a kind of synthesis that we witness in the High Middle Ages, particularly the thirteenth century. Learning for now consisted of putting the sources together, meager as they were, and giving attention to the incessant need for the hand copying of manuscripts. "Originality," as the modern Westerner thinks of it, was scarcely possible. John Scotus Erigena, the Irishman of the ninth century, stands out as the notable exception. He first translated the works of a Neo-Platonist named Dionysius (late fifth or early sixth century), but also added some metaphysical treatises of his own. However, he had no successors, at least not for some time. As tenacious as the monasteries were to preserve and invigorate learning, societal and community conditions often placed severe limitations upon these valuable but vulnerable islands of scholarly work.

The disarray of the collapsing Carolingian world in time gave rise to a new monarchy, the Ottonian dynasty. The rulers issuing from this dynasty, more or less took the feudal society as the new world, but this by no means meant that they accepted their world as it was. Moreover, in 962, a Germanic king named Otto led his soldiers in a resounding defeat of the previously menacing Magyars, an antecedent peoples of the Hungarians. He thus seemed to fulfill his claim to be the successor of Charlemagne. He went to Rome, as Charlemagne had done, and was crowned as emperor by Pope John XII in 962, as Charlemagne had been in the year 800.

Otto, called "the Great," certainly seemed as impressive as his notable Frankish predecessor. Moreover, Otto was notably ambitious and this Saxon German emperor now prepared for his successor son by managing to betroth that son to a Byzantine princess. It is natural to see in this ruler a continuation of the rule and aura of a Charlemagne, both positively and negatively, for Otto's son and grandson in particular, were far less able rulers than their father and grandfather, Otto the Great. In this they resembled Charlemagne's familial successors. On the other hand, however, the alliance developed between the Ottonian rulers and the Church resulted in a stronger political state. The emperor and the pope worked in a reasonable union in the best of times, but sometimes locked in contentious battle.

However, there were cultural differences manifested across the burgeoning regional map of Christendom in Europe. Just as the Byzantine East was differentiated by a mass of details from the Latin West during the medieval period, so too the Latin West was noted for the differences manifested in its conglomerate of varied cultures. We might therefore justifiably note the southern Roman culture of Italy and Rome, for example, and the Frankish/German culture of the more northern regions of Europe. The culture of Italy and Rome represented classical values pronounced by their genesis in the Roman inheritance that grew out of the classical world. Here, one might say, form and function were important, and judgments grouped around the notion of fitting established understanding. For example, the architecture of the Romans hung on in the Romanesque style of building. Here there was a great wealth of learning and experience to be drawn upon in the present, which sought, for the most part, to model the past.

The notions of invention, creation and problem solving, however, seem to belong more to those cultures, like the Frankish and the Germanic, that found themselves in situations requiring some deviation from the past, in part because their past is different from the past of a rich classical society. The values of this culture might and will be assimilated to the Christian values upon conversion, but such a culture is also aware of its particulars and will be attuned to making a new blueprint, rather than just reading an old one. This culture, therefore, might have more dynamism at its center, and portend the tendency toward original and even reforming movements. Nevertheless, the new Gothic style of architecture of the north will be accounted as the style of barbarians by southern Roman and Italian culture for some time. The tag of "Gothic" still carried connotations of barbarian, except now these "Goths" were beginning to close something of the cultural gap between the old and the new.

Partly within such differences, we can witness political or national differences that serve as telescopes for the nearing next steps of the medieval period. That is, France and England will begin to build monarchies that in time compete with the whole edifice of the empire and the Church. Meanwhile, the Frankish kingdoms of Charlemagne and the line of the Otto's from the Holy Roman Empire are still vying for a unified Christian society or state.

Even the squabbling between the pope and emperor could hardly nullify the aspiration for unity, however bumpy the reality. When Otto in 963 contested for the right of the emperor to extract an oath of loyalty from a papal candidate aspiring to be pope, he was asserting his authority over that office. However, papal subservience had its limits even in the bond of church and empire. In 1076, as a result of the Gregorian reform of Pope Gregory VII, an attempt is made to reverse the kind of relationship Otto had crafted between pope and emperor. Moreover, when the king of France moved the papacy to Avignon in 1309, or when Henry the VIII of England much later pushed the papacy outside his own monarchy, that was quite another matter. National churches would be the culmination of these kinds of assertions of independence.

Trouble was also brewing deeper down in society at the lay level. That is, if the institution of the Church and its ambassadors had managed to salvage something of the classical and Roman inheritance, in doing so it also kept itself from the average citizen and Christian, who remained virtually as illiterate as his tribe had been centuries earlier. When we come to Charlemagne, however, we do see a concentrated attempt to raise up not only scholars, but to raise the literacy level, starting with ordinary parish priests.

After Charlemagne, however, there seems to have developed some resentment on the part of monasteries to educating laity who scarcely looked like people who would be entering the monastery. Therefore, as this was virtually the only place besides cathedral schools where these kinds of skills could be taught and acquired, their removal boded ill for raising up significant numbers of literate laity. Coupled with a lack of means for education was the additional problem that the language of the empire and the Church was Latin. This single language boded well for those who had a hand in the running of these institutions, for it provided ease of communication across a host of differing cultures and national tongues that would have been virtually impossible but for the common language. However, it also meant that a two-tiered society based on a difference of language forced those ignorant of Latin to stay beneath the higher rungs of a society. It is no wonder that hopeful parents prayed for their sons to enter the offices of the Church. Here was virtually their only route to a life and living better than the one into which they were born.

Charlemagne's immediate successors turn monasticism more in the direction of ascetic ideals than educational edifices. With the fall of the Carolingians and the tumult of that transition, the ascetic propensity is boosted by the weariness of a society fractured in a variety of ways. Therefore, the solace of the monastic and ascetic life began to draw upon hungry souls who now wanted a disciplined regimen that provided some comfort for them in a wayward and warlike world. Such appetites would generate a revival of sorts that placed monastics at the forefront of piety but also of power.

MONASTICISM GROWS

At the end of the first decade of the tenth century, a modest monastery was launched in northern France, but from it grew within a mere century the largest network of monasteries yet seen in Europe. Cluny by name, this order placed itself within the womb of Benedictine monasticism, but with significant differences, not to say advances. With a foreshadowing of the Gregorian Reform to come in the next century, these monasteries were under no lay supervision. Such places managed to operate free from interference from lay leaders and also notably, other clerics. This order was subject only to the pope. Some of its leading members offered welcomed counsel to much older Benedictine monasteries. The Cluniacs noticed that the work of monks had changed since the time of the founder, St. Benedict. By this time, monks rarely engaged in physical labor for financial necessities. Rather, they increasingly were the intermediaries for lay society through the administration of liturgical rites, while also providing limited educational opportunities as well as exercising some political influence. While free of lay control, the Cluniac monks willingly accepted donations of property and other endowments for financing the functions these monks provided for the community at large.

MEDIEVAL CIVILIZATION

As the Cluny reform spread, so did a new spiritual emphasis that infiltrated members of lay society with a spiritual exercise that almost continuously gains ground among the faithful in the ensuing centuries. Though the great monastery at Cluny and its liturgy and its building stones were impressive and wondrous to those who managed to witness this complex, the Cluniacs and wider community of those in monasteries were not seeking to honor saints in monasteries. Rather, during this period the practice of making a pilgrimage became increasingly popular, and while there were many places serving as destinations for such journeys, in the northwest corner of Spain, there was a special place. In the Compostela Cathedral were reputed to be the remains of one of the disciples of Jesus, James. This destination had pride of place in the medieval period for pilgrims. Indeed, spiritual fervor was markedly directed toward material things in this time, and so the exalting of relics or things of historical significance were esteemed among the communities of the faithful. Understandably, the things of most significance were things associated with Jesus or close to him, which drew people in the present toward the adoration of the remains of things from the Christian past. These kinds of things possessed meaningful significance for the faithful, who deemed them advantageous to their spiritual journey.

Fruits of the Burgeoning Medieval Civilization

Therefore, they were sought out, and in time, monasteries and churches became rich repositories of relics.

Pilgrimages, however, were even more special to the faithful. On a pilgrimage, one undertook a physical journey that served as compliment and analogy to the spiritual strivings of religious life. Furthermore, because the Christian religion was an historical religion, it was rooted in particular persons and places and things that remained a part of the sacred past, even as those material things suffered the ravishes of time. Here one could grasp or seize something of the eternal in the temporal present, and the relic or place was of such significance that the practices growing up around these things attracted more than monks and clergy, though certainly them too. Soon stations of rest or facilities for encampment cropped up alongside the most popular routes of pilgrimage. Understandably, then, enterprising trade would grow up around such a venture.

In more ways than simply its organization, Cluny contributed to a kind of internationalism in a period of Western medieval history when the fragmentation of society into fiefdoms and the like seemed to have localized the activity and world of most people. Networks of spiritual practices, however, now came to extend over wider and wider terrain, so that some of the population did have some acquaintance with the outside and larger world. However, it is certainly the case that trade during this period did for the most part confine itself to local transactions. The far flung trade routes, such as the vaunted Roman roads and even the mysterious Silk Road were reduced and neglected in much of this period, so that what a family and community had access to was largely constrained by their locality. As vast trade networks shrunk, trade as a way of making wealth became difficult over distance, and so estates, and sometimes vast estates, reminiscent of the older Roman estates, bind their wealth to land and property.

An economy that is virtually constrained to its local area, therefore, will almost of necessity be a barter economy. Connections for trade to faraway places being lost or trimmed, the means for financial transactions across cultures or bodies of water becomes largely unnecessary. This diminishing of economy and international trade, particularly in an east-west direction, has been traced to the jolt of the Islamic presence in and around the Mediterranean beginning in the seventh and eighth centuries. The contentiousness between the Christian and Islamic cultures was not kind to exchange, for hostilities between the two religions significantly lessened prior ties of trade in Mediterranean traffic. With trade in the south of Europe encumbered by the Islamic visitation, trade shifted northward, but there was less of it, for the bridges of prior economic and trade networks, for example, with the Byzantines, were already attenuated. With the addition of Islam, therefore, there is in effect a trade blockage that in future centuries subsides, but it was a contributing factor to a slowed or stalled civilization that now had to hunker down for having lost some of its prior assets. Therefore, providing for the safekeeping of wealth prompted landed wealth—there were simply few other opportunities. If the menace of ever increasing barbarian infiltration into the old Roman Empire had precipitated the fissure of many Roman country estates of earlier centuries, in the new European economy facing less international trade, there was an increase in landed wealth amassed by the nobility.

Other historians have argued, however, that though the Islamic presence was a significant pressure placed upon Europe and its economy, particularly in the locality of the Mediterranean, the West had endured other pressures, such as those of the Germanic tribes and the unfriendly coolness of the relationship with the Byzantine East. The net effect of such pressures, though for a time desultory, nevertheless pushed Europe into a civilization significantly different from competitors. In a way, like Gregory the Great had surmised centuries earlier, the West would have to make, or better said, invent its own way. In subsequent centuries observers would witness this weak conglomeration of cultures catapulting itself into eventual ascendancy over others.

One reason for the popularity of the pilgrimage to Compostela in northern Spain was simply that the Islamic presence was sufficiently south in Iberia to undertake the trek to the north and Compostela in relative safety. In the northern regions of Iberia, the Christian population had managed to contain further Islamic advance. Nevertheless, the reminder that formerly Christian lands were now no longer in Christian hands must have pained the faithful. The liberation of the lands in Iberia would be a half millennium in coming.

In the Islamic advance, the Christian West had also lost much of the geographic areas of New Testament Christianity, including Jerusalem. To Jerusalem, Christian pilgrims would still come, just as they would to Santiago. However, Jerusalem could be a journey imperiled by more than the usual dangers of travel in such an age because it was in the hands of a competing religion that occupied lands once in Christian hands. This thought would invigorate counter aggressions that would ultimately be responsible in time to come for launching the Crusades, but that venture, while enjoying some initial successes, managed to retain no long term successes or territory. Like the effort of Justinian the Great to retake lands from the barbarians centuries earlier, these enterprises were much more expensive in terms of lives and other costs and produced few actual benefits.

REFORMERS AND MARAUDERS

Meanwhile, the number of monasteries and Cluniac monks and the size of endowments grew steadily. The aesthetic of the liturgy, as well as the architecture of its buildings and like characteristics, vaulted this order and its members into prominence. Kings and other rulers were its willing students and devotees, and the notable Emperor Henry III (1046–1056) was a patron of the order. Part of the reason for such alignment between the crown and clergy was regal approval of the Cluniac insistence that clerical orders and priests be purged of abuses. As political leaders often had a substantial hand in affairs of the Church, churchmen naturally preferred lay leaders to be sufficiently spiritually orientated themselves. However, noticeable were cases where lay and political leaders exceeded religious leaders in their spiritual discipline and concerns. As scandals sometimes developed over the occupant of the papal office, Emperor Henry, as example, took upon himself the task of sorting out competing popes, as each denounced the other as unfit for the office. Amidst the problem of revolving papal claimants, there was also the problem that popes, like the great mass of medieval people, sometimes were very short lived and thus frequently came and went rather quickly. The intervention of a political ruler into these kinds of religious decisions would later become suspect, as later clerical attempts to reform the Church would question the role of lay leaders as spiritual authorities; for now, this same Henry appointed his cousin to the papal office as Leo IX.

Like his lay cousin Henry, Leo too set himself to the task of restoring order and morality to church and society. Perhaps most notable about this pope was that he noticed an inordinate amount of persons of Roman heritage serving as papal advisors. Such a group would in time be referred to as cardinals. Though the new pope was himself a German, Leo nevertheless now rounded out the occupants of high Church officials to include a variety of tribes, now conceived as nationalities. New blood being inserted into the hierarchy of the Church set the Church and its organization on one plank of a serious path of reform, in a way that the older patrician Roman families, from which many popes had issued, resisted.

The Church would now be subject to renewal with serious and not infrequently combative reformers at the helm. Understandably, some changes would create much tumult in the Church and in the political sector. Some emperors, as, for example, Emperor Otto III, presented themselves as something of Constantianian rulers, which of course created some anxiety among Westerners suspicious of the East. What was cobbled together in such an effort, however, would soon emerge from the Ottoian accomplishments as the fabled Holy Roman Empire of the West. However, just as this was happening, something significant would change for the direction of the future, as the lands of Italy and the papacy would look back to the center of civilization as drawing them toward the Mediterranean. The future of the formation of Europe, however, was gravitating toward the north, as Islamic armies continued to chisel away at vulnerable Italian and Roman provinces in the south of Europe. The future of Europe was moving toward later cultural and religious division within Christendom.

The Islamic advance, by reaching into the depths of Iberia, would eventually reveal to Western Christians what resources Islamic scholars possessed. Indeed, the Frenchman Gerber, who would become Pope Sylvester II (999–1003), had studied philosophy and mathematics with Islamic teachers in Spain. It was later rumored that this eventual pope manifested the power of sorcery because of the company he had formerly kept. Gerber, moreover, found himself the teacher for Otto III, before becoming Pope Sylvester II, at the age of around fifty.

If King Arthur and his Knights of the Roundtable are historical mirages, King Alfred the Great of Britain is not. The rulers of his Wessex were substantially linked with Christianity before him, and in 871, Alfred managed to hand the Danish Norsemen their first defeat in a vulnerable England weakened by their marauding. His successes, though not always constant, did manage to provide for retaking London itself. Perhaps equally impressive, and reminiscent of Charlemagne, Alfred infused a renewed quest for learning. Furthermore, aware of the distance of the common man from Latin learning, he noticeably placed some insistence on alternative learning in the vernacular. Therefore, not only texts in Latin would be copied at his court. The real benefit of such a ruler would only become greater after his death in 899, though Danish assaults would continue. However, because much of the Viking population had been Christianized, the enormous

Fruits of the Burgeoning Medieval Civilization

change of a defeat at their hands was not as disruptive as the first visitations of the Vikings had been to Europeans.

With many marauders eventually subdued and slowly incorporated into the Christian overlay of a tribal and fragmented but eventual Europe, the papacy would now assume more and more primacy in Europe. However, there was almost always a community of lay political leaders with whom negotiations were imperative as seen in Otto and Henry and others. Moreover, the Ottonians, as example, pushed and pulled popes as if they were in charge of the Church. In later ages, however, one would see some future emperors humbled and humiliated and excommunicated by their presumed papal partners in the making of a Christian Europe. Nevertheless, for this time period, the Ottonians had intervened as willing correctors to a papal office sometimes running amuck. When the load of the work of the Church at the highest levels could not count on disputed or double popes, bishops beneath could only thank political interventionists for sorting out the highest office, while they did the work below. In this way, some clergy and indeed some monks, might have considered the possibility then, though more acutely centuries later, that the political sector or its leader or leaders should be in charge of the religious realm.

CHRISTIAN ADVANCE AND SPLIT

The struggles to see the Christian religion into the far reaches of Europe, such as Scandinavia, would remind one of the earlier struggles of that religion to establish itself in the Empire after Constantine. That is, though sometimes kings of the various Viking tribes would show support for the new religion in their realm, a successor king might mount opposition to Christianity. By about the year 1000, Christianity had a fairly firm foothold in the Scandinavian lands, except for Finland, which would require another two centuries. In Eastern Europe, Hungary and Poland came slightly before the conversion of the Scandinavians. These countries assimilated themselves to the Latin or Roman Church, but the Eastern or Orthodox Church did not remain still. In fact, Bulgaria and Armenia were subjugated by the Eastern Empire at the turn of the millennium. The Bulgarian czar was baptized in 864, and the Bulgarians and the people of Serbia and Romania came into the Eastern Church.

An interesting case is that of Moravia, located in the eastern portion of the modern Czech Republic. Two brothers, named Cyril and Methodius, from Greece, set out for Moravia in the mid-ninth century. They translated the Bible and conducted the Eucharist in the language of their converts, rather than in Latin. Word of this tactic reached some German ears, and petition was made to the pope in Rome to bring them into line with Latin as the language of the Church. Though Pope Adrian II (867–872) permitted the brothers to continue as they had been doing, that decision was overturned by a later pope, and followers of the two Greek brothers went to Bulgaria and became Orthodox instead. The insistence upon the single language for conducting services within the Roman Church was not something that the Eastern Church would require. The prior case of the emerging nation/state of Bulgaria poised Catholic and Orthodox in a frenzied hostility at times.

Because both the Eastern and Western Church took seriously the missionary message of Christianity, they frequently came into contact and conflict with one another. The entry of Islam into Europe had pushed Christian missionary activity particularly toward the northern sectors of central Europe, and still today, along with Islam, we can discern the religions of various people that were decided in the centuries around the end of the first millennium.

During this historical time, kings decided the religion of their people. Nevertheless, this did not mean such a decision was made lightly or was only a personal decision. Rulers must have made some calculations of prudence for which religious body to opt with, and some would have considered something of the temperament of their people and potential alliances with neighboring peoples or kingdoms. In other words, undoubtedly some of the same considerations that prompted Constantine and then Clovis to move toward this religion now reappeared again, with these later groups of people coming into the folds of the Christian religion. The Romans and the Franks and Germans, to speak only of the West, were now vying for new people to join themselves to the Christian religion that the Romans, Franks, and Germans had joined in past centuries. Certainly for a king, the political considerations might understandably loom largest, but these considerations alone were not the whole story.

The assimilation of the vast country of Russia to Christendom is perhaps such a story. In this country, the prince of Kiev begins to consider an appropriate religion for his people. Christian missionary activity had been present in this huge area for probably two centuries beforehand, but had not made significant inroads among the people or leaders. Aware that

Fruits of the Burgeoning Medieval Civilization

Christendom was not all of one piece and ever aware of the closeness of Islamic religion, he decided to send ambassadors out to investigate the possibilities of a religion fitted for his Russian people, which might include Islam.

In 987, the ambassadors went out with orders to bring a report back from their observations about the religions. In what survives as a record, it appears that an aesthetic appeal made the deciding difference to these fact finders. They reported back to their leader that the impressiveness of the Christian liturgy witnessed inside the great Hagia Sophia built by Justinian the Great completely shattered anything else they had seen among the competition. So the Orthodox faith became the religion of the Russians, and the next year Vladimir, the eventual Vladimir the Great, married the sister of the emperor at Constantinople. In all likelihood, the strong empire of the East was as important to Vladimir as the impression of Orthodox worship was to his ambassadors.

However, if the Western Church and its organization and its *lingu franca* of Latin retained and furnished the few opportunities for learning and advancement in the medieval period, by contrast the Eastern Church appeared lavish and steeped in a suppleness grossly lacking in the poorer and coarser West. Thus, even if the Eastern Church could permit another culture to retain its own language in biblical translation and the rite of the Eucharist, those who possessed the Greek oftentimes looked from above and askance to those below who did not because they could not. Moreover, if at times the Eastern Church and empire perceived itself as aiding the weaker Western Christian brother, the East at the same time perceived the West and its nation/cultures as roguish with unlettered leaders. Indeed, to present Charlemagne, as the West did in 800, as an emperor when the Christian world had an emperor at Constantinople, was virtually treasonous. From the perspective of the East, in such a move as this, the roguish West was showing its rebellious streak.

Most of the eventual nations of central Europe went the way of the Orthodox rather than the way of the Catholic Church over the language issue and the proximity and strength of the Byzantine Empire. What is apt to be missed in this debate, however, is that the insistence upon the universal use of the Church's Latin by the Roman Church was not always characteristic of the officials of the Roman Church. Gregory the Great, for example, had advised Alcuin, his missionary to England, to within reason allow local and national customs to remain with the new Christian religion among the converted English. However, a different Roman Church practice later may have to be explained by more than a change of popes. In other words, it may have to do with emperors exerting themselves into theological disputes, as we saw Constantine do. Thus, to some historians, it has seemed like the decision of one language for one church, though of many nationalities, might appeal as much or more to an emperor than to a pope. Here again, however, we can see that the influence of the political ruler into more than politics might raise the eyebrows of popes and clergy. In this manner, then, those reformers producing the eventual Gregorian reform begin to wonder who is running the Church.

So perhaps the Carolingian connection to the papacy had worked against the Church. Certainly we can observe Charlemagne, reminiscent of Constantine at times, running ahead of the Bishop of Rome on theological decisions. For example, Charlemagne, not the pope, condemned the Second Council of Nicaea called in 787 to heal the strife over iconoclasm in the East. Indeed, Charlemagne's legates produced some volumes after the Council that showed little sympathy or understanding of the issues involved. Nevertheless, to Charlemagne and his successors it might have seemed that Eastern differences would be tolerated at the price of unity or a unified empire.

The papacy in this time would become increasingly cognizant of how powerful the emperor of the West had become. Whereas Charlemagne's immediate family predecessors and his earliest successors had been welcome participants in forming the Christian Church and society, now they were wielding power enough to be dangerous. Though the differences and friction between Eastern and Western cultures and churches were obvious, the papacy nevertheless wished to maintain good relations with the Eastern emperor. This was simply because the pope might need a Christian brother as an ally in any struggle with the Western emperor.

From the papacy would now come both requests and rebukes. As a way to have everything desired, the papacy offered to support the Orthodox emperor in exchange for the patriarch at Constantinople submitting to the pope in Rome. Significantly poisoning realistic possibility for any agreement, however, was the fallout from two letters in transit to Constantinople. Both were written by the Roman pope for Constantinople; one letter was for the emperor and one letter was addressed for the patriarch. The letters and their reception have marked for many the formal historical separation of the Western Church from the Eastern Church.

Fruits of the Burgeoning Medieval Civilization

The letter for the emperor was kindly and respectfully worded; the second letter for the patriarch was abusive and unmerciful toward the past history of struggles between the two churches. The pope had sent his friend Cardinal Humbert with the letters to hopefully negotiate the terms of any agreement. Though a Cluniac monk, he had none of the persuasive powers of one, and in fact, appeared rude and obstinate. Coming armed for every possibility and after an atmosphere of unpleasantness had transpired, the cardinal and his party strode up to the high altar of the Church of Hagia Sophia during a service and placed the papal excommunication of the Eastern Church on the altar. As if this were not enough, on leaving the building, they dusted any Byzantine dust off their feet, while an indignant crowd hurled abuses at them. The year was 1054.

5

From the Heights of Medieval Civilization, 1054–1347

GREGORIAN REFORM AND MEDIEVAL EXUBERANCE

The centuries beginning with the Carolingians reflected a time when, however slowly, nobles and kings and emperors began to establish some dominance over vast areas of what would become Christendom. Aside from the agreements and alliances between an emperor and a pope, such partnering in power was not satisfactory to reforming popes of the eleventh century, nor were existing religious orders sufficiently rigorous for some new monastic orders created in this period, as, for example, the newly minted order of the Cistercians. This order, and its most prominent leader, Bernard of Clairvaux (1090–1153), would criticize severely the reforming Cluniacs as not reforming enough.

The most noticeable events of this period began with the efforts of a papacy intent on reform to establish dominion over political leaders, however pious and well-intentioned some of these political leaders were. It ended with some kings competing with the power of the papacy and in some significant instances kings not losing in a confrontation with a pope. With some justification one might allege that it was precisely the work of emperors such as Otto the Great, who by their assumption of power to depose unworthy popes, put themselves on notice to aspiring papal reformists. If such emperors had done their job well, reformists contended that it was not their job to do. In effect, the reformist party did not desire any shared religious power, for such power belonged to churchmen, not to mere laymen, whether princes or emperors. Such a working model for the work of the Church necessarily drew fire from political rulers and may have backfired on the movement for reform. That is, it provoked some to begin to theorize in radical and even proto-modern ways about the relationship between the religious and political components of society. Some even began to tinker with what authority the population as ordinary people might possess.

By the time of the Fourth Lateran Council in 1215, the religious establishment of Europe would lay down directives about how to proceed in a new social and intellectual climate. The great Western universities that are with us still today were brought into being during this period. In a significant way these universities and their conflicts are portends of the future of Christendom and the culmination of the Middle Ages. Among the most significant persons of this period appear figures from the greatest university of the youthful universities, the University of Paris. Many of the first scratchings of some modern ideas and institutions are thus provided within an epoch some medieval historians have gauged as the most resourceful period of the Middle Ages. Therefore, this time has not unnaturally been referred to as a Renaissance or Reformation before the later historical events usually awarded those notable descriptions.

Historians have referred to a part of this period as the "Gregorian Reform." The namesake, Pope Gregory VII (1073–1085), did not act alone, but in his twelve-year tenure as the pope—known to many as Hildebrand—he was extraordinarily active on the stage of the European world of

Christendom. Indicative of calamity issuing from opposition to his reform attempts, he died in exile—driven there by a retaliating imperial force.

During the political reign of the Carolingians and their successors, the rule and authority of the Church and the state had sometimes melded. Gregory, however, regarded this as a wrong relationship and relied heavily upon St. Augustine's distinction between the City of God and the City of Man to distinguish the realms of the Church and its authority from all else. Like Augustine, Gregory looked upon the state as an institution for serving the godly purpose of attempting to restrain evil. The state was therefore a servant of God's purposes for the world as ultimately reflected in the Church. Necessarily, then, the state should stand with the Church, but behind it, and not in front or even beside it. To give some empirical reality to such a claim, Gregory remarked that the number of kings in eternal felicity since the origin of the world could be counted on perhaps one hand. By such an assessment of the subservient heritage of the state coupled with morally tainted leaders of the state, Gregory was putting the political world in its proper place.

Congruent with this thinking, Gregory also opened up new forms of spiritual life and piety by shifting attention away from kings and nobles and people of high station in life. Drawing attention to the "poor in spirit" and the frequently attendant poverty accompanying them, Gregory showed his ascetic side and indeed his puritan sensibilities. People of means therefore were hardly his ideal mean for the Christian pilgrim in this world. This form of piety and spiritual life was one purged of the lavishness and often licentiousness of regal ways. Therefore, the ordinary laity could approach the throne of God as easily, indeed, easier than those who sat on thrones in this world. This kind of inversion of thinking, however, would understandably make much of this epoch contentious. Popes after Gregory would uneasily contain religious orders who espoused poverty, for example. Gregory in effect supported a piety that some later popes would not infrequently fear and resist.

The soaring cathedrals built during this time are often interpreted as symbolic of the summing up of the High Middle Ages in all its grandeur. While this may explain the impetus of such magnificence, their effect may have been greater, or even of a different kind than the reason they were constructed. That is, ordinary people began to have a more visible place in the medieval period. Such magnificent buildings do represent what might be called high culture, though the cathedrals as distinct from monasteries or convents gave particular physical form to the piety of the ordinary parishioner who frequented it as he sought a place for his soul and the plight of his earthly struggle. The common people must have stood in awe of such spectacles as they were being built, and as extraordinary achievements, they for the most part remained part of the landscape for generations and centuries. However, as tall as the spires of the great Gothic churches might go, these magnificent buildings surely put worshippers in a mood of elated devotion compared to earlier and smaller, darker structures. The greater light and expanse inside these churches made possible by the massive and illuminating windows was symbolic of a laity now coming more alive and to some degree becoming more powerful in the life of the Church. The laity would come to light, but if the light in the Church dimmed, they might turn elsewhere. Significant theological deviation, or heresy, would be another feature of this period.

Certainly there were critics of such magnificence as Gothic churches exuded, as simply too ostentatious and thus distracting and therefore no ally for spiritual purposes. The most prominent critic of this distracting lavishness, whether in architecture, or clothes, or ceremony, was Bernard of Clairvaux. Bernard thought sensual accompaniments to spiritual devotion would soon provoke abandonment of the latter for the delight of the former. He was a severe critic of the Gothic spectacle undertaken at St. Denis in the Paris region by Abbot Suger (1081–1151) and urged his Cistercian monks to avoid the sensual distractions common to the weak souls of men. The Cistercians, by living in what began as waste lands in remote places of Europe, could manage this kind of aesthetic austerity, at least for a while. However, the powerfulness of Bernard's personality and preaching and writing drove him to be politically influential and not a remote figure. Bernard was influential on the stage of world events in his era more than perhaps any other person in any era of the Middle Ages, excepting of course some popes.

NEW CRITICS, NEW ORDERS, NEW LEARNING

Greater than Bernard of Clairvaux in terms of a more enduring legacy was Francis of Assisi (c. 1181–1226). This man is probably the individual most associated with the medieval period by casual spectators of the Middle Ages and with good reason. Even the twentieth century Voltairien Bertrand Russell complimented Francis as one of the sweetest individuals ever having lived. Bernard, by contrast, was not infrequently confrontational and overbearing. Both men and their different personalities are nevertheless illustrative of some common features of this slice of medieval time.

Bernard came from a family of the nobility in Burgundy in France, while Francis was the heir of a cloth merchant in Italy before he disowned his earthly inheritance for his inheritance in heaven. Bernard did not create the religious order of Cistercians he belonged to, but he did grow its numbers exponentially starting with several members of his own family, and something about this order is lacking if its most famous member goes unnoticed. By contrast, Francis was severed from his family, but created a religious order largely because his winning personality had made magnetic appeal to many. While Bernard preached the Second Crusade in 1146 that turned out very badly, St. Francis preached to the Islamic Sultan of Egypt in 1219, though too, without success.

From the Heights of Medieval Civilization

The particular piety of both men placed them at significant cultural distance from the rise and notoriety of emerging scholars in the new universities that in time would be called scholastics. St. Bernard, moreover, drew himself into famous controversy with a notable scholastic, Peter Abelard (1079–1142). Bernard believed scholastics were bent on knowledge for the sake of vanity, though perhaps for some, unconsciously so. Nevertheless, for the seriously religious or Christian thinker, such was simply and at best an exercise in idle curiosity. Bernard was interested in probing the spiritual riches of the Christian message, and to that end, he studied the writings of earlier Christian thinkers—the Church Fathers—not the scholastics.

In a culture with scholastics such as Abelard, Bernard became suspicious of the enterprise of thinking for the sake of thinking, even if it were thinking about Christian things or ideas. Bernard wanted a Christian piety that resonated with and produced religious fervor that made for godly lives. To Bernard this was remote from the minds of scholastic thinkers absorbed with questions treated by the intellect. Bernard was unimpressed and critical.

Moreover, disagreement over knowledge and Christian knowledge was part of much earlier debate, extending back to the initial decades after the Christian Church came into existence. Sitting on the cusp of ancient Greek and then Roman civilization, the earliest thinkers of the Christian faith had placed themselves at various positions over rejection or assimilation of these intellectually impressive traditions. Augustine, as we saw earlier, contended that some of the preceding traditions had provided historical stepping stones for and to the Christian message. Nevertheless, though intellectually curious, Augustine was not primarily interested in thought or thinking for its own sake, but he was intent to find and savor what mattered between men and God. Others, however, like Boethius, had attempted to bundle up and assimilate prior traditions for Christian use.

Still others like the North African thinker Tertullian (c. 160–c. 235) had retorted to the question with his own question made famous by his wording: "What does Athens have to do with Jerusalem?" So as to make the point of contrast even stronger, he interjected, "I believe because it is absurd." However confrontational such phrasing may be, the question remained for thinkers who were now Christian thinkers, about how to treat legacies of the past in terms of the Christian present.

St. Bernard thought that knowing must be put to the use of Christ, and while this program had an obvious practical dimension, it also meant that the mystical route to knowledge might plumb the depths of God better than the cerebral competition from scholastics as arrogant as Bernard thought Abelard. Indeed, what was amply wrong with Abelard and the scholastics in the mind of Bernard was their use of tools for thinking about God and the mysteries of God in the same way they did for any other subject. For Bernard, Christian thinking was not just thinking about something that was different, as Tertullian had reinforced with his question, but it presented something that was to be thought about differently.

For reasons like these, some monastic traditions accentuated a chasm between themselves and the scholastic traditions. This breach in Christendom would remain permanent for the future, though some medieval individuals had a presence in both traditions. Many later and modern secular thinkers looking back to this debate would simply conjecture it about the choice between knowledge and its opposite. For people like Bernard, and to some extent Francis too—and before him Augustine—the debate was rather about what grounded and strengthened the relationship between God and men. Not infrequently, this perspective referenced the contention of St. Paul the Apostle to the Gentiles, that in Christ are hidden all the treasures of wisdom and knowledge. This way of thinking almost necessarily gave invitation to mysticism. By the thirteenth century, mysticism began to flourish, but at about the same time, the first fledgling moments of scientific thinking also began to appear. The age was rich in the invention or reinvention of things old and things new.

If the Cistercians, represented by Bernard, were intent to focus attention on nothing superfluous, like the emerging and visually tantalizing Gothic architecture of the age, and though some lived as recluses by living in remote and out-of-the-way places, they sometimes carried great political weight nevertheless. Bernard best exhibits this in a life given to great mystical enhancement of the Christian faith, but also by being actively involved in the world, to the point of advocating his preference between competing candidates for the papal office. Historians have sometimes surmised that Bernard had a split personality; he was a man of the world and not of it.

Francis, by contrast, never wanted to be party to political machinizations, property, or prosperity. Francis's Gospel was the simple Gospel of doing Christian work without fanfare or accolades. Nevertheless, the stringency of living the Franciscan way caught the attention of the papacy. Comparisons of the two usually invited perceptions of contrast, and the papacy inevitably suffered.

From the Heights of Medieval Civilization

Whereas the crowning of Charlemagne by the pope in 800 represents for many historians a subtle jockeying for power between two powerful individuals and offices, something of the same conflict surrounds Pope Innocent III (1198–1216) and the verbal sanction he gave to the Franciscan way of life in 1210. Unlike the case of a pope and emperor, however, Francis was not in competition with Church hierarchy, but was an obedient and dutiful servant of the Christian message. This pope in some measure, nevertheless, surely feared Francis and so too the Franciscans precisely because the impressions of them would sometimes impinge negatively upon the material and spiritual state of the papacy. Therefore, Francis and his order would be respected by the papacy, but fairly soon after the death of Francis conflict developed within the order itself over whether to keep and maintain the stringent requirement of poverty. The Church hierarchy noticeably sided with the party that would relax such stringency.

Unlike the rural Cistercians, Francis and his order worked the villages and cities, in part because this is where people tended to be. Here they preached and evangelized, and like Francis himself had done, urged those rich in material things to turn their eyes toward the state of their soul, rather than their house and belongings.

Unlike the puritan inclinations of a Bernard to contract some of the sumptuousness of worship and the life of Christian devotion, the earnestness of Francis took the form of expansiveness. That is, whereas the Cistercians lived in remote corners and the Franciscans in population centers, Francis nonetheless found something of a spiritual communion with and among other created things, most famously, birds, the moon, and the sun. For Francis, the message of salvation was for all creation, and thus he took his preaching beyond the human population to nature. Francis was not extravagant, he was charitable, and part of his charity was to surround the Gospel message not just with the choirs of heaven or humans, but with all creation and creatures. It is easy to judge Bernard as dour and someone sometimes dreaded by his acquaintances. Francis, however, seemed as enabled by Christ as anyone living for Christ might live. More, he seemed supple in his extension of the Christian message beyond the range of his predecessors.

After him, and starting with St. Bonaventure (1221–1274), who, after his stint as a professor at the prestigious University of Paris, assumed the reins of the Franciscan order in 1257, the Franciscans produced some very notable and famous thinkers, to include Bonaventure. Two more of them,

Duns Scotus (1265–1308) and William of Ockham (c. 1287–1348/9), were the leading thinkers of their age. In fact, the "nominalism" of William of Ockham would occupy the stage of debate for decades after his death.

Because of the propensities of Francis, his order was attracted to nature and this necessarily drew some of them into the direction of a study of nature. This is why, among some of the most notable thinkers scratching out the beginnings of modern science, we find Franciscans such as Roger Bacon (c. 1213–1294). However, as important as a study of nature is for the start of science, equally important are the conceptual schemes used to classify what is seen and witnessed. It is here that the role of William of Ockham's nominalism becomes pertinent. From it derives the famous "Ockham's Razor."

Ockham gave primacy to the individual or the particular in the context of knowledge. That is, to some degree, Ockham removed conceptual hindrances to knowledge by insisting that the individual instance is the starting point of knowledge, not the conceptual scheme it may share with similar instances. The value of this perspective is that it may enable an observer or scientist to see the individual for closer to what it is, or said stronger, as it is, if the accoutrement of an interpretive scheme is laid aside. Another way we might express this idea is to say that knowledge does not begin from the top by looking down, but from the bottom up. Somewhat like Pope Hildebrand, Ockham felt the need to turn things upside down to get them right.

St. Dominic (1170–1221), founder of the Dominican order, is often rightly compared to Francis and the Franciscans, simply because both orders were dedicated to poverty and both orders were also mendicants. Because the practice of mendicants was to beg for their necessities, this almost necessarily put both orders into urban environments. Differences between the two founders and orders soon became apparent, however. Whereas Francis had famously preached to the Islamic Sultan, Dominic had been sent as an Augustinian canon and priest to preach among some of the theological radicals in the south of France, called the Cathars and Albigenses. Though his efforts were largely without success, he surmised from his experience that theological education was imperative for such work to succeed. Thus, the order that took his name developed into an order devoted to learning and teaching. Along with this emphasis and because of it, the Dominicans would lend aid to an Inquisition attempting to right some wrong thinking of individuals and groups not going the way of the Church.

NEW HERESIES

In sectors of France, particularly southern France, some itinerant preachers had preached a message undermining much of conventional religion and practice. These preachers were for the most part fierce critics of things like relics, pilgrimages, and even crucifixes that were judged as not just superfluous distractions from proper devotion to God, but often strongly condemned as idolatrous. As if such ideas were not radical enough, some of these preachers came close to absolving the Christian need for a priest, and in more severe cases, a minister at all. Despite the individualistic emphasis of such teaching, substantial groups and communities emerged around these ideas and eventually provoked the attention of religious authorities.

Such preachers might with justification be compared to the attractiveness of the early Christian message for persons living in the empire who felt something vital missing in the rather formal attitudes and ceremonial worship of the Roman gods. Into this vacuum had stepped the so-called mystery religions, Christianity among them, and within this latter religion, individuals were attracted because the message of Christianity seemed to address cravings to which Roman religion did not stoop. A God who had become human provided a humanistic religion in threading an identity between God and men in the God-Man Christ.

For critics of the medieval religion of this period, the space between God and men became likened to ever-increasing clutter as piety took on a myriad of ways and often unusual forms and directions. The simple Cather and Albigensian preachers enunciated with various degrees of clarity that much of this enterprise amounted to clutter and should be removed as trash. The institutional church and many of its practices obviously came up for criticism from this perspective. Different than the conflict that St. Francis posed for the Church, many of these radicals presumed what amounted to the real Church within or outside of an apostate church. Clashes would be inevitable.

And the clashes came. Though slow to react in the beginning, officials eventually employed debates to confront the menace of these radicals. However, the tenacity of these new preachers and their followers hung on adamantly, and eventually would produce one of the most notorious of all medieval institutions and practices—the Inquisition.

RISE OF THE UNIVERSITIES AND CONTROVERSY OVER ARISTOTLE

The Dominicans, with their emphasis on education, also had a part to play in the rise of medieval universities. Their most famous member, Thomas Aquinas, was a professor at the University of Paris for a time. Most of these budding schools started rather humbly, and in the beginning would not be recognizable to our age which associates buildings and a campus with education. Virtually all educational efforts growing out of what amounts to the High Middle Ages were overseen by the Church and its directors. However, political leaders also began to charter such establishments. Moreover, though it was a theological age, and the subject of theology was touted as "queen of the sciences" in such a culture, the religious atmosphere did not prevent most things, subjects such as medicine and law, from being taught. In addition, because the religious culture of the age revolved around the Bible, the ability to read was one required skill, but more than simply reading words was necessary to comprehend the meanings of scriptural stories and the latent theology of this great book. A fuller education, therefore, had to acquire some competence in a myriad of subjects.

Prior to fledgling universities, education had been undertaken under the aegis of what were called monastic schools. The work of education in the aftermath of the chaos of the barbarian invasions had largely stopped, except for monasteries which by default tended to store and copy and then accumulate books. However, literacy was scarce in such ages, even among many of the monks. Some living in the Carolingian era, however, had seen the great need and had put into place some provisions for education. At first of course, education was intended for their own, or clerics, but also moved to some aristocratic houses or families where record keeping and other such matters demanded at least some basic literacy.

There would be tracks in the universities portending the later fissures of modern universities emanating in a secular direction. The reception of the corpus of the Greek thinker Aristotle to the Latin West provided the occasion. As was also the case with Plato's writings, the West had suffered in prior centuries from a scanty inheritance of Greek writings. Visitation to Islamic Spain, however, had made some Latin scholars aware that though Aristotle was lost to them, his works had not been lost to everyone. However, the tedious work of translators was first required for reading what had been preserved by Islamic thinkers. For the philosopher that Thomas Aquinas honorifically called "The Philosopher," cautions would be voiced by some but enthusiastic reception accorded by others. The debate over how to incorporate this thinker's thought with reference to what the Christian religion and Church taught would prompt considerable strife, particularly in the classrooms of the youthful universities and, of course, from the highest echelons of the Church.

Plato's philosophy had rather easily commended itself to religious thinkers who saw in this thinker a step toward the transcendent world of God in heaven. Aristotle, by contrast, was more of the earth and appeared rather distant from the main orientation of medieval religious thought compared to Plato. However, it was not simply the case that Aristotle was the thinker who upset the applecart of medieval thinking in this period. It was rather that many thinkers around this time, though certainly gaining impetus from considering Aristotle's concepts and explanations, began giving credibility to conceptual schemes that sidestepped theological considerations. Theological study might present possible additions to knowledge, but was fundamentally unnecessary for it. In an age which was strongly religious, this tendency or belief had to be muffled, if not muted. Thinkers of this sort aligned themselves with a radical group called "Latin Averroists." They asserted that their claim to knowledge was one based solely on human ingenuity and natural understanding. They took their conclusions from their reasoning powers, but offered the caveat that any conclusions were inculcated and protected from errors by the life jacket of concessions to or deference for divine revelation. This last point was viewed by many as simply a sop thrown out to satisfy the theologians and more religiously-minded, who would mind a claim that looked like a claim for human autonomy. But the die was cast, and from this point forward, what in time would become autonomous and secular thinking would be placing its foot down regarding knowledge purporting to be theological in origin. Philosophy was beginning to assert its independence from theology. Thinking will began to claim independence from religious thinking.

Some of the beginnings of this struggle can be seen in the difficulties of two notable professors who would need the aid of the papacy to be allowed to teach at the prestigious University of Paris. This was in part because they were monks, or more accurately friars, a Franciscan and a Dominican. The Faculty of Arts at Paris, from which Averroism most issued, protested these two mendicant friars as recipients of university chairs. The two, St. Bonaventure and St. Thomas, maintained a friendship between them, despite their significant differences over what to do with Aristotle's thinking in relation to Christian thought.

Bonaventure's stand with reference to Aristotle's thinking was cautious, not to say indifferent. That is, the limitations of this pre-Christian thinker were so evident and everywhere noticeable, that to use some pieces of his thinking, valid though they might be, was cumbersome enough to perhaps question why use him at all. Bonaventure did not think Aristotle expedited understanding, particularly Christian thought, to warrant speaking of his philosophy with such glorious adjectives as his admirers described him. Bonaventure reflected much of the Augustinian approach, mixed in with the Church Fathers, and suffused with enough mystical openness to cast some shadow over the rational approaches of many of his contemporaries.

Thomas Aquinas is appropriately thought of as one occupant of the highest pinnacles of medieval thinking. However, one must exercise due care with such aplomb because to some, his *Summas* was deemed overextended. That is, the sheer size and many contentions made them vulnerable to formidable critics.

Thomas, however, though heavily using Aristotle, is not slavish toward him, but now he will have to endure some of the same kind of criticisms of his more radical colleagues because of his use of Aristotle. This is in part why, in the Condemnation of 1277, only three years after the death of Thomas, among the many highlighted theses anathematized by the document issued by the Bishop of Paris, there are some attributed to St. Thomas. There are more, of course, attributed to the more radical Avveroists, which proves the point that while the immediate issue was Aristotle, the deeper issue was what to do with philosophers whose reliance and respect for theology was perceived to be weakening. For some years after the issuance of this document, Thomas's Dominican and other followers and students kept their heads down.

Thomas's two best known works are his *Summa Contra Gentiles* and his unfinished *Summa Theologiae*. The former is more the nature of a work of apology or defense of the Christian Catholic faith. Furthermore, Thomas lectured on the books of the Bible while at Paris, and his commentaries on some of the latter are easily missed by focusing on just the scholastic Thomas. He even wrote a few hymns that are still sung in Christian services today. Typical of a mendicant friar, he was not just an academic, but as a Dominican, had many duties. His last duty was a journey to a meeting at Lyons, France, in 1274 in the effort to bring the Western and Eastern

Orthodox Church back together after the 1054 fiasco. He died on the way, however, and it is crude evidence to the great man that at his death, the monks at Fossanova, Italy, desiring a relic of him, boiled his corpse so as to have their wish. Some days previous to death, however, he had what appears as a stroke, at the age of around forty-nine, and with it he lost nearly all of his faculty of speech. His secretaries traveled with him, and anxious that he return to finish work on his *Summa Theologiae*, one secretary ventured that suggestion to him. Eventually, he did manage to speak, but only to indicate that what he had hitherto written "seemed as straw." Shortly afterward he died.

Legion are the interpretations of the nearly last words of this great medieval thinker, and they reflect the variant interpretations of what he accomplished. To someone earlier, like Bernard of Clairvaux, little of real use was accomplished by the scholastics. To others—like a Catholic tradition that would proclaim in modern centuries to come that St. Thomas was the touchstone of Catholic philosophy—Thomas was a careful and Christian thinker who could show successors how to navigate the turbulent world of ideas and remain Christian in the exchanges and endless debates of the intellect. For others, he stretched the Christian faith over a philosophical system, largely that of the empiricist Aristotle, and in so doing, may have bent it out of its original shape. This is not to say that he made a religion into a philosophy, but rather that in some details, he may have implicated the Christian religion into secular streams of thought that would in time disavow it. For example, Thomas's preference for Aristotle's notion that the human is a social being and that community is essential to what a human is, stands in contrast to Augustine's notion that the existence of a state is brought about because of the calamity of evil in a sinful world and the need to restrain it. Similarly, Thomas presents a detailed trajectory of how knowledge comes to be with no necessary or even needed reference to God. Augustine, however, included God explicitly in his notion of how humans develop their ideas and grasp truth. With Thomas and his successors, the possibility emerges that religious truths or ideas may lose their distinctively religious clothing simply because their coherence with reason justifies or explains their cogency without needed reference to religious faith or religious truths. Philosophy may be accessorized with religion or without it.

Nevertheless, we can lose our way in all of this if we forget that Thomas's more radical colleagues were on the cusp of regarding theology as something of an irrelevancy to doing philosophy. This is why they can talk about their contentedness with Aristotle alone; nevertheless, Aristotle owed every bit of his philosophy to his own natural faculties and none to divine revelation.

Here we meet William of Ockham again, though not for the last time. Ockham gave little validity to the philosophy that theologians like Thomas had affixed their systems to, for this radical Franciscan affirms the idea of the radical freedom of God. This means that God is not shackled by anything the philosophers had foisted on his being or his activity. The knowability of God, therefore, only comes about from the biblical revelation God sends to us, and not the chain of reason the philosophers had used to presume to understand the ways of God. We only know with reliability about God, what God tells us in special revelation or Scripture. The Averroist, by contrast, who is suspicious over any claims to knowledge from that direction, will be forced back onto his philosophy for his theology.

RISE OF NATIONALISM AND THE VERNACULAR

The desire of Pope Gregory VII that the pope run the Church began to crumble anew when French kings came to increasingly compete with the power of the papacy, just as, the nobles of King John of England were forcing their king into submission to the famous Magna Carta. Despite the dislike of the very powerful Pope Innocent III (1198–1216) for King John (1199–1216), Innocent nevertheless took the side of the English crown in vilifying that concessionary document.

Elsewhere, the Eastern Church and the Western Church would descend to a new low in their already tattered relationship. The Fourth Crusade, 1202–1204, though successful, was a disaster within the kingdom of Christendom. Largely composed of French troops, these Crusaders made negotiations along the way that turned them toward Constantinople. Though Pope Innocent tried to prevent this diversion to the glorious city, it happened nevertheless. The Crusaders not only worsened the unstable political situation there, but they manifestly helped themselves to the riches and reliquaries of the splendid city. This calamitous visitation of the West upon the East is still etched in the memory of the Byzantine East and the Orthodox Church. Added to this insult, with Latins in charge of Constantinople, the Greek Church was in subjugation to the bishop of Rome or pope. Though regaining Constantinople in 1261, the weakened empire of the East would now limp along, with its prior glories largely past.

From the Heights of Medieval Civilization

If Pope Innocent III represents the apex of papal power—by his ability to cow kings and other parties—his successors, chiefly Frenchmen, made the officers of the Church more and more French. Furthermore, however chaotic the regional leadership of Europe at this time through many unfit political aspirants, some political leaders in time did begin to wrest control of their fiefdoms, now kingdoms, and then aspiring nations, from the papacy. The French and the English are the most notable examples. Germany by contrast was in much disarray following the ferocious contest of power between the Hohenstaufen German leaders and the papacy. Thus, from the mid-thirteenth century until the time of the Reformation, the weakened states within the once-strong Holy Roman Empire limped along.

The rising sense of nationalism in England and France prodded the peoples within to think of themselves as English or French, and to think of the pope, particularly if he were Italian, as a foreigner. However, in the contest of wills between their leaders and the papacy (There was ever only one pope who was English), what was often at issue was money. In the protracted Hundred Years War between France and England, the need for money tempted and then prompted these kings to tax the clergy in their respective countries. The clergy understandably complained to the pope about such subjugation, and in 1296, Pope Boniface VIII (1294–1303) drew up a papal bull prohibiting any such action from a king, on threat of ex-communication. The French king issued a counter edict of his own, which had the effect of lessening papal power and provoked grudging acknowledgment of regal power from the papacy. The English King, Edward I, received a similar though again a grudging concession from the pope. Unlike past centuries, national leaders could now stand up to the papacy and sometimes win.

In 1301, a showdown between Pope Boniface and the French King Philip IV (1285–1314) began, and the end result was a humiliation of Boniface by placing him on trial. The pope did not budge, but the ordeal killed the hapless man a month later. With Philip in effect now in charge of the papacy, the seat of the institution was moved in 1309 to Avignon. While the papacy stayed at Avignon until 1377, every pope was French.

Thus it was that William of Ockham was summoned to appear before the pope in Avignon in 1324 to answer some questions. Ockham this time was taking the side of the Spiritual Franciscans concerning the issue of poverty. In 1328 he fled Avignon in the company and protection of an uncertain sort, from the excommunicated German Emperor of Bavaria, Ludwig IV.

In addition, the Franciscan General, Michael of Ciensna, was with them. The controversy over poverty with the Franciscans was enough to make the erudite Franciscan Ockham suspicious to the papacy. Moreover, that controversy had pushed Ockham into writing political treatises. In them, he exhibited more of his prescient modernism with his contention that the state should be independent of ecclesiastical jurisdiction. Another prominent figure of this circle, and also under the arm of Ludwig IV, was Marsalis of Padua. In 1324, Marsalis had written his *Defender of the Peace* in light of the struggle between Ludwig and the pope. Marsalis was an Averroist of sorts and had also been a teacher at the famed University of Paris and rector of that institution in 1313. Controversy over what Marsalis wrote in the pages of his book fanned debate for a century and met with the sternest rebukes from the papacy. Marsalis dared to venture various contentions that jolted much medieval thinking, such as that Peter was not the greatest or most privileged of the Apostles and that a council (or conciliarism) carried more authority than the pope.

However, it is with the name of Dante Allegrihi that observers of the Middle Ages are most likely to surmise the grandest summation of medieval times, that is, up to the lifetime of Dante, (1265–1321). This qualification, moreover, is needful, for what we generally refer to as the "High Middle Ages" are thought to have ended sometime around the mid or late fourteenth century. Moreover, even in Dante's summary, we can rather easily discern that there are flaws in the medieval fabric that in future generations will become rips and tears. That being said, there have been multitudes of competing interpretations of Dante's story, not least of which are debates over who and where he places various historical figures within his epic tapestry.

Not to be left unnoticed about such a writer as Dante, given his monumental project, is that he wrote in Italian, not Latin. Like some of the authors of his time, he tended to write in both languages, but the newer language, the vernacular or national language would in time take more and more places where only Latin once ruled. This took some time, however, for other writers of the period of Dante, such as Petrarch (1304–1374), retained a love of Latin. This single difference between the two men can mask the fact that even though a close reading of Dante's *Divine Comedy*, and particularly his piece *Monarchy*, reflects a man aware of the debates of his time, the writings of Petrarch reflect the thoughts and image of a man yet to be. That is, Petrarch reflects his Renaissance image; Dante, struggling ever

From the Heights of Medieval Civilization

so dimly toward the future, reflects something of an embattled medieval man, but still a medieval man. Petrarch, by contrast, portends the future.

6

Fall and Descent of Medieval Civilization, 1347–1517

THE BLACK DEATH

What is commonly referred to as the Black Death ravished most parts of Europe in the mid-fourteenth century. By the death of so many hands, a labor shortage necessarily occurred and this removed land from cultivation. At virtually the same time period, the so-called Little Ice Age disrupted and diminished crop yields and food reserves further. The plight of the masses of ordinary people was one virtual constant afflicting the medieval period, and the aftermath of the Black Death added more despondency to the lives of many. Despite the frequent susceptibility to starvation and the near lack of necessities for life, the medieval period could be one that was extraordinarily community minded. That is, while the extent of this varied by region and century, and while class differentiation was certainly pronounced between the strata of classes, the Church, and in time the culture it came to influence, took care of more than simply their own.

However, in the aftermath of the Black Death added strains produced conflicts and rebellions. Some incidents were precipitated in part because a general rise in wages owed itself to increased demand for labor and workers, in light of fewer population numbers. This naturally gave workers for the most part some benefit, but also some confidence that may have provided stimulus for individual and social initiatives scarcely thinkable before. In other words, something of a better life and world for the worker made the worker begin to expect more, not less, but even less so, to be simply content with his lot.

Secondly, taxation began to rise during this epoch, to a significant degree because of the financing of wars. This is particularly so with reference to the Hundred Years War between England and France. Over the issue of taxation, moreover, was animosity toward the benefits of clergy who paid little to no taxes. This, coupled with the expansive Church lands, steadily created envy on the part of lay populations. Therefore, sectors of the population harbored some hostility for both the regal and religious classes.

The ravages of the Black Death and periodic reoccurrences also trimmed the population of monastic communities as it had the population numbers of lay communities. Nevertheless, lay people criticized what seemed to many as luxuriant or idle living among monks professing the spiritual benefit of poverty. A fair amount of satirical literature during this time focused on what was deemed the hypocrisy of some religious orders. On the other hand, however, some of the remodeling of monastic facilities, to take one example of criticism of the orders, was probably undertaken as advertisement for traveling and paying quests. Indeed, in a time when an economy was strained by fewer workers and rising wages, the monasteries needed ways to replenish their purses. The Cistercians, noted for their employment of lay brothers to undertake the manual labors of land reclamation and cultivation and other such tasks, found the new times difficult. It was hard to find and to pay workers after population reduction coupled with the rising wages that new workers expected.

Therefore, increasing perception of laxity among religious and monastic orders contributed to the disgruntlement of lay populations. Indeed, the lay population may not have exercised its religious devotion with any more energies than neighboring monastics, but a member of lay society still expected, as he did of his church in the parish and from its center in Rome, evidence of setting a moral example. He was quick to spot and then judge a lack or lapse.

Revolts by peasants and others were not particularly common during this period, but some of the revolts carried noticeably intense conviction. In addition, though the characteristics of these revolts and the people carrying out these revolts was different by nation and region, in general, the attempt was to eradicate serfdom. However, the composition of the protestors sometimes included members of the gentry and occasionally clergy. Probably the most notable revolt is that of 1381, sometimes referred to as the English Peasants' Revolt.

Though beginning in the area of Kent, it picked up willing accomplices along the way, primarily from counties of the southeast of England. The rebels get a concession from the English king, the youthful Richard II, to eradicate serfdom, but later this is retracted by the king, and many leaders of the movement are killed. The historical significance and meaning of this much scrutinized incident is still debated today. Though usually claimed by socialists, research has revealed that there was a conglomeration of people making the protest and included some persons of substantial means. Furthermore, some of the areas from which the protestors came had witnessed a level of increasing prosperity that would have been the envy of those from other areas of England not engaged in similar protests. Coupled with the new-found betterment, these persons nevertheless remained strapped to a political system detrimental to their further advance. Indeed, when some of the protestors found an audience with their king, their appeal was one in which they seemed to assume something of a popular sovereignty for themselves. This indicated the need for removal of intermediates such as the lords. Further, the complicity of some monastics as it concerned property rights was another and significant bone of contention for laity. This episode of revolt ultimately failed, but it was a herald of things to come in the approaching modern world.

Thus, the medieval world began to point toward the focus of a future world or society in which the planks of freedom and equality would eventually become installed, at least where popular sovereignty or democracy was intended. In the late medieval world we can glimpse some of these things being birthed as ideas, but both are stalled in the harsh realities of the medieval world. However, the modern world is sometimes assumed to have birthed itself into modernity. Nevertheless, in this period we find movements and emphases which are harbingers of things to come in the Western world.

THE ADVANCE OF MYSTICISM

When Innocent III in the year 1208 contended that there was no salvation outside the Church, this in effect meant both structurally and doctrinally. While political rulers and emperors might have been the intended aim of this document, it also placed boundaries on doctrinal deviations that would be most in evidence when the Church dealt with theological deviation from lay populations. The Cathars and Albengians, however, in effect aimed at both the structure and the doctrine of the Church, though of course different groups gave varying emphasis to where they laid their charge against the existing Church. Mystics would also be some worry for Church authorities, though they were certainly not always rebels. Mysticism could be and was incorporated into the thinking and lives of great intellectuals, such as was the case with St. Bonaventure and others who managed to combine a perhaps rather arid scholasticism with the warmth of mystical feelings. Sometimes, such as in the case of St. Bernard of Clairvaux, one encounters a fierce critic of the scholastics and at the same time a fierce critic of forms of piety that do not reach the inner being for which Bernard was aiming. Thus, Bernard is an example of a person who might have inadvertently driven devotes into seeking forms of piety more fulfilling than those found in the existing Church.

Mysticism might be described as privatized religion, but this characterization misses the intensity of the mystic. In the West, the seriousness of the mystic generally assures the mystic of some or even great respect, but to religious authorities, the intensity coupled with the prestige often presents a problem. Religious authorities may ignore the mystic, but to do so is usually to their peril, both positive and negative.

The mystic might be perceived, rightly or not, as closer to God than the echelons of leaders above him. If this perception is the perception of the mystic himself, he is probably tempted or prone to haughtiness or arrogance. If, however, this is the perception of others, then officials may be leery of the mystic, however humble and dutiful he may be, as usurping or diminishing their authority whether intended or not. The Franciscan order, with their emphasis upon a piety of poverty, provide an example of this possibility. That is, some of the fear of the papacy was that in contrast to the Franciscans, the papal office and legates and other Church officials might appear quite worldly by comparison.

The other fear of mysticism in the medieval period can be exemplified with the example of St. Francis himself. As seems abundantly clear, Francis was not beset by pride, nor was he attempting to show up others by his own devotion. Moreover, the story goes that Francis during his lifetime received the stigmata, as indication of his devotion to Christ. The stigmata took the form of receiving the wounds of Christ as Christ received them at the Crucifixion on his wrists and his ankles. Despite the extraordinarily remarkable character of such an event, Francis avoided public show of his wounds, nor did he clamor about his closeness to God in receiving the stigmata. Thus, Francis does not substantiate either of the two greatest fears over mystics. One is a sort of arrogance which might stand ready to forego the Church or its structures or rituals as unnecessary for religious life and devotion. This had largely been the fear of the Church over the Albigenses and Cathars. Francis, by contrast, was an ever-devoted and obedient son of the Church. Some of his followers, such as William of Ockham, however, would take issue with the Church. On Ockham's stand for the Franciscan Spirituals, Francis would have quietly acquiesced with Ockham's judgment. However, on Ockham's view of the relationship between the secular and religious realm, Francis might have desisted.

The second fear, also unrealized in Francis, is that in achieving closeness to God, the mystic might cease to refrain from any comparison to God, believing himself to be one with God. The usual complaint against this kind of close affinity to God is that it smacks of identity and thus, is too near monism or pantheism.

As population numbers increased after the ravages of the Black Death, religious women became larger in numbers and significance. These women represented part of the common yearning for a lay piety of sorts. This in part was also prompted by disaffection over the leadership and failings of Church leaders. The Beguines were a particularly notable group of lay women sometimes associated with monastic orders, but most of the time found living in the traditional setting of a family. Their piety was noticeable, however, and they exhibit evidence that spiritual movements such as theirs were prepared to work in the world in new ways anticipating a later time. For example, they often worked in lay occupations taking care of children or worked as essentially garment workers. They did tend to find and even organize communities around themselves, which of course, brought them to the attention of Church authorities. As religious heresies seemed to be proliferating during this period, the eyes of the inquisitors were watchful.

Moreover, because they were unmarried, many of these women simply looked for something productive to do. This seems especially the case with females from the higher classes and some that were daughters of nobility. Membership from these sectors of society often precipitated incorporating an order of females alongside the established male orders, like the Cistercians. Females from the lower classes tended by contrast to be less establishment oriented, and therefore invited quicker accusations of theological deviation from Church authorities. Nevertheless, the line between what was orthodox teaching or behavior and what was not, was not always easy to determine. Though the parameters were clear for the most part, there was always room for some ambiguities. The implication, whether conscious or not, must have often been to stay within the safety of the Church. There were obvious dangers befalling those too close to boundaries. Thus, any reform movement stood a far greater likelihood of success if formed from within the Church, in contrast to movements which sprang up among laity whose connection to the Church seemed much more tenuous—as evidenced by their radical criticisms.

SOCIAL AND THEOLOGICAL CRITICISM OF THE CHURCH

An undercurrent of social criticism of the Church nearly always existed alongside the religiosity of the medieval period, though of course more present in some periods than others. Probably the most notable of such persons was Erasmus of Rotterdam (c. 1466–1536), who on the eve of the Reformation was unsparing in his criticism of some religious practices and even popes who had desecrated their office and the religious life of the Church. Earlier there had been some works still well known today by the names of *Piers Plowman* and *Canterbury Tales* that present a ribald humor over stories of religious extravagances and sheer dupery. Written in vernacular language, such works reflect what many of the illiterate of the day must have seen and felt. The undercurrents of such works and many lesser pieces were some of the first stones cast at a Church and culture gone somewhat arrears.

With the monstrous captivity of the Church still pedestaled at Avignon and the papacy not returning to Rome for good until 1377, there was much disgruntlement with the formal Church. Moreover, there was still no agreement about the best way to select a pope, and this confusion and chaos took a tremendous toll on the respect of the ordinary medieval person for his Church and Church officials. For some time, critics of the papacy had contended that the ultimate authority for the Church should be invested in a group rather than the single individual of the pope. This theory or movement of conciliarism, as it was called, reached its apex in 1414–1418 at the Council of Constance. While the Council did succeed in removing the multiple claimants to the papacy, the declaration concerning conciliarism was not formally approved. What was approved was the condemnation of the thought and theologies of two pre-Reformation thinkers, John Wycliffe and Jan Hus.

The contentions over a papacy then living in Avignon and multiple claimants to the same office of pope drew a variety of critics. Notably witnessing the former states of affairs from across the English Channel was John Wycliffe. At almost the same time, the Italian Petrarch (1304–1474) was yet another critic, but a critic different from Wycliffe. That is, both men contributed to different streams of thought, but comparing the two also reminds us that the famed Italian Renaissance was not permeating the rest of Europe when it was starting to establish itself in places like Florence. Indeed, Wycliffe and others began a movement that would anticipate the later Protestant Reformation, whereas the Italian Renaissance would in part anticipate later modern and secular culture. That being said, however, both streams and tributaries to the streams do sometimes cross. Thus, for example, the sensual Florence in the decade of 1490 fell under the spell of the puritan Dominican preacher Savonarola, who persuaded the Florentines to dispose of their art and their infatuation with art and build fires over it; for a time, they acquiesced. Medieval reformers like Savonarola could still be heard raising their voices amidst the new culture of the city, but it would not last, and in 1498, Savonarola was a victim of the same fires and the same people who had burned Florentine artworks under his direction.

NEW WORLDS DISCOVERED, THE JEWS CONSIDERED, AND THE WORD RECONSIDERED

In a few more months and in the year 1500, the Portuguese explorer Pedro Alvares Cabral discovered Brazil. Suddenly the medieval world was discovering other worlds. Indeed only a few years before, Pope Alexander VI, to prevent more calamities between the Spanish and Portuguese, drew a line across South America intended to define what was the province of Spain and the province of Portugal, and most memorable to generations of Western school children, Christopher Columbus discovered the Americas in 1492. Usually missed, however, is that this date is also the year in which the last Islamic bastion at Grenada was retaken by European Christian armies. Columbus's good fortune at the hands of Ferdinand and Isabella was, no doubt, in some part due to the elation of leaders who saw the Islamic intrusion finally conquered after a presence of seven centuries in Iberia.

The Western world was itself about to expand hugely as it extended itself geographically to new lands. That is, it would also be changed within as the budding experimental procedures of some late medieval thinkers advanced to produce the underpinnings of what would eventually become modern science. The changes wrought with this change would be extremely influential upon the foreign cultures that the Westerners would visit. This is to get a bit ahead of our story, even though Columbus certainly did bring impressive armaments to the places he visited in the new world compared to what the host population possessed. However, he and many other explorers brought something else not possessed by the host population: the Christian religion. As much as the appetite for new land and new trade routes appealed to sovereigns financing exploration at the first steps of the rising modern age, as indication of the medieval inheritance, the Christian religion still carried great cultural weight. Even so, however, there were initial fears in the religious fabric. The proliferation of mystics was but one indication of a wall now beginning to crack. The scholars and new scholarly methods would be another.

John Wycliffe (1328–1384) was an English academic theologian. In time Wycliffe's reputation extended beyond his own Oxford, and eventually he contributed to the political debate over when a disreputable ecclesiastic forfeits his position by reason of his offenses. Some of the political factions in England saw the worth of such a position in contention with a Church only too prone to protect and favor its own. In such an instance, unlike in the popular estimation of the case of the martyrdom of the churchman Thomas Beckett at Canterbury (1170), the royal authority might have had the better position.

Meanwhile, Wycliffe began to ink criticisms of the Church that would have a significant future. That is, while Wycliffe did not abjure the papacy for its right to office, he clearly laid down principles that would significantly change the way the Christian Church thought of itself and its members and leaders. When he turned to attack the doctrine of transubstantiation, he received his most sizeable opposition, and many defections from his camp followed. His opponents linked Wycliffe's criticisms with the English Peasants' Revolt of 1381. Thereafter his movement, which came to be called "Lollardism," weakened.

It would find legs outside of England, however, for in the year 1383 King Richard II of England married Anna, a Bohemian princess. Such marriages of regal persons were the order of the day, for the linkage of desirable kingdoms, one to another, was achieved in such a fashion. This marriage, moreover, put English thinking into the ears of some Bohemians, and it was not long before some scholars in Bohemian Prague began to read Wycliffe. Some, such as Jerome of Prague, even went to Oxford University to study. In time, what fizzled and went underground in England as Lollardism arose in Prague.

What the leader of this movement from Bohemia and the movement after him managed to accomplish must surely have been the quiet envy of other parts of Europe. However, it would take the martyrdom of the leader, John Hus, (c. 1369-1415) and a population incensed by the manner of his trial at Constance to mount an effective resistance to the Roman Church. The movement, labeled "Hussite," dared to give communion in both kinds to the laity—this for many observers became the trademark of this Church. So successful was this bloody rebellion that this group—in effect fighting for a national and autonomous church—assumed its place as such within the humbled Roman communion. Naturally the latter did not concede this willingly, but concede it, it did. Nevertheless, in 1462, Pope Pius II nullified any such concession. The Bohemians, however, remained proudly unique in Christendom for possessing more liberty on religious matters than most any other Church in the West.

People of Jewish faith had constituted perhaps as much as one tenth of the population of the Roman Empire, but in a medieval and broadly Christian culture, the relationship of the predominant Christendom to the religion from which it had sprung grew increasingly contentious in the second millennium. The relationship between the two religions had always been uneasy, but this was more or less dependent on the region. Compared to other regions of Europe, Iberia had an unusually high proportion of population that was Jewish. Those who were wealthy tended to be greatly resented, particularly in the financial sector, as the Jews engaged in usury, something disdained by the Church. Nevertheless, their financial services were used because they were needed. However, in the time of the Black Death, Jews came in for hard scrutiny from the wider Christian population, who claimed to suspect them for the calamities associated with this scourge of disease and death. The tendency to mysticism, as a type of introverted withdrawal, was in the ascendency as pressures and persecutions against Jewish populations mounted. This form of Jewish mysticism came to be called Cabbalism and was aided by Jewish thinkers suspicious of some of their own who seemed to have veered too much toward a rationalistic approach to deity, as they surmised some Christian thinkers had. One Jewish thinker of note, and also influential upon St. Thomas Aquinas, was Moses Maimonides (1135-1204). Though born in Spain, he left there for fear of the Almohades Muslims, who offered conversion or death to those not Muslim. He first went to Morocco but finally to Egypt, where he found some solace.

As persecution of Jewish populations increased, more and more Jewish persons migrated eastward to Eastern Europe and particularly the Baltic region. Their plight in Iberia increasingly worsened. In 1492, those Jews refusing to convert to Christianity were expelled from Spain. Previously, the rulers of Spain had been pressured by the Inquisition to do so, and a very large number of people made the exodus, many of course, to their death. Portugal, however, would hesitate until 1497. The Portuguese king recognized the human resources that would be lost in replicating the Spanish event and managed for a time to dither. A sizeable portion of the Jewish population did convert under the constant pressure to do so, but many managed to discreetly maintain and practice the former religion. They were called the new Christians. When pressures became too much, often Jewish families would leave for cities like Amsterdam or London.

For the most part, the Jews had fared well in Spain until ousted, but the expulsion from that land was seen by them as one of the worst cases of being turned out of a country. The cause was the insistence by the Spanish crown that lands in Spain be unified in Christian belief; this is why we witness the Inquisition in Spain wielded not by the Church, but by a state feeling itself responsible for the health of the Church. Even the papacy was hesitant to intrude too much into Spanish affairs, and in 1496, Pope Alexander VI conferred on Ferdinand and Isabella the title of "Catholic King and Queen" for their fervent piety.

As pointed out by many historians, the Jews were without qualification among the most literate and educated people of medieval times. The unique opportunities this provided were fairly extensive, but also the envy of many others. Expulsions, especially such as those of the 1290s both from France and England, represented huge cultural loses to the nations forcing the departure. Migrations from these nations tended toward Germany, from which the Yiddish variant of Hebrew developed.

MEDIEVAL IMPLOSIONS AND EXPLOSIONS: SCIENCE, WEAPONRY, AND THE TURKS

Mixed into the late medieval populations are the names of people who would henceforth become famous in laying much of the groundwork of modern science and technology. Copernicus, who was Polish and born in 1473, would be among the first to reconfigure the layout of the cosmos, and others would engage in experimental enterprises that would bring about the modern conception of the universe. About this same time, the printing press would revolutionize the speed with which ideas could be disseminated. Henceforth, with the invention and steady improvement of this technology, communication and mass communication in particular, would become possible. People began to see printed things as they had never seen before, even if levels of literacy amongst the population were still abysmal.

Of course, the great Bible would be the book amongst books most desired and coveted among a religious population. Ironically, the religious culture that esteemed its reception and struggled with its precepts would now begin some shift toward the steps of a secular culture. The contrast between Machiavelli (1469–1527) and Joan of Arc (1412–1431), though she lived about a century before Machiavelli, exhibits this kind of contrast between a religious culture and a culture drawing near to the secular.

However much Joan would be the heroine for Frenchmen of her time and many others later, in significant ways she was politically naïve, in part because of her mystical bent. Her authority, though coming through the voices heard, was nevertheless strongly rooted in the Catholic Christian tradition. She brought alongside her faith strong devotion to her nation, as was the case with the political leaders she stood with and those she stood against. Her patriotism and her piety were not compartmentalized, but all of a piece.

With Machiavelli, things were quite different. Religion and religious belief and religious persuasion were all well and good for Machiavelli, though this is perhaps a bit of an exaggeration in describing him. Machiavelli puts religion in its place, and for him it has its place, which largely means its uses. Any purposes it serves are for the maintenance of power; ruling a people is about ruling a people with the means available. Machiavelli is often referred to a pragmatist without principles or without deeply held principles. However adequate this might or might not be to describe his thinking, there is something rather banal or every bit as brutal as the worst of the Middle Ages in his political philosophy. Machiavelli is therefore scary to some, but scarcely a hero, though he tells his readers how a prince can maintain the image of a hero; Joan of Arc, a heroine, provokes our sympathy, for however idealistic the young woman was, she is deemed as standing for principles worthy of more respect than political cunning or political survival. She is at least a bit reminiscent of a Socrates, unafraid and determined because of the things she places higher than her own life. Machiavelli, however, simply desires and plans for his prince to be left standing at the end of the day. For him, cumbersome metaphysical explanations or justifications need not be attached to morals; indeed, morals need not be attached to power, except in so far as the perception of such a union is thought to be necessary to gain and maintain the support of a population.

St. Augustine, contemplating the reasons for the diminishing power of the Roman Empire, considered that Rome's spiral into weakness was because it never produced a sufficient reason to be, aside perhaps from its initial aim toward being a republic. Thus, Rome was simply powerful because it had the resources—and some policies, to be sure—to be powerful. Rome served no end greater than itself in the end, and this is part of the reason Augustine thinks it fell into essentially a dictatorship.

Medieval thinkers and particularly some Renaissance thinkers began to reminisce about the glories of the prior classical world. When later modern science will began to trace its antecedents to some of the earliest Greek thinking, such as that of the pre-Socratics, the Renaissance complaint against the Middle Ages of being surrounded by two giants seemed vindicated.

Furthermore, just as science resumed some progress, invariably coming with it was enhanced technology. Probably one of the most noticeable examples to late medieval people would have been warfare technology. The romantic knight in shining armor, though a fit subject of poets and tale bearers, was scarcely fit for the battlefield after the invention of extended pikes. With one of these long and fearsome weapons, a man on the ground could make short work of a flailing man on horseback. Improved crossbows used skillfully by archers could bring the same man on horseback down easier than the man on horseback could ever hope to launch his spear at the archer. Most important, however, was the beginning use of gunpowder, borrowed from the Chinese. With it, cannons could be made to fire at castle and fortress walls. As a consequence of this new vulnerability, walls had to be made thicker or present angles that could deflect the smashing balls.

Gigantic and destructive balls would break the previously impenetrable walls of Constantinople in 1453. Such weaponry came from the Ottoman Turks, a group of Islamic peoples who in the early part of the century had surged into the once Christian territories of Serbia and Bulgaria. Pushing toward the prize of the enviable city of Constantinople, the Turks had laid seize to the city in 1422, but had to withdraw because of other commitments. However, the rightly troubled and scared population knew that a return would be fatal for the city and it was, two decades later.

Fall and Descent of Medieval Civilization

The Byzantium kingdom of the East had been in something of a free fall for a couple of centuries. Striving to raise itself back up to its former glories, it sought alliances that would hopefully bring reunion with the Roman or Western Church. All such attempts, however, were pitted against the unquenchable memory of the fourth Crusade that had sacked portions of Constantinople in 1202 and then had inflicted Latin rule for a time on the Greek Byzantines.

The inevitability of the Byzantine fate in the face of Muslim advances seemed so assured, moreover, that the last emperor, Constantine XI (1449–53), over the strong objections of his Eastern Church officials, was willing to grant Rome concessions that his churchmen could not stomach. Moreover, in prior centuries, the Western Church had made attempts to reunite the two churches of the East and West. Rome had called a council, referred to as the Second Council of Lyons, in 1274 toward that goal. Indeed, it was toward this Council that the great philosopher Aquinas was headed when he died on the way. Bonaventure, too, was called to this meeting. However, little was accomplished and Constantinople would be ripe for the picking by its Islamic adversaries. In 1453, a canon so large and heavy arrived at the sought city after a journey that could only advance two and one half miles per day. Having positioned the weapon within range of the fortified gates and walls, the Turkish commander asked for surrender, but no reply came. With his new and monstrous weapon, he beat down the previously impregnable walls faster than the Byzantines could repair the damage. In May of 1453, the Turks took the most coveted city of the world. In the aftermath of this colossal blow to the East, some Russian leaders began to assume some of the previous leadership supplied by Constantinople. The Russian known as Ivan the Great married a niece of the last Emperor of Byzantium in 1472, and soon the Russian leader would be referred to as the Tsar, a Russian term for Caesar.

The threat of Ottoman or Turkish Islam would not recede, for fears grew that this force would bore deeper into Western Europe. What had been regained by the Reconquista of Iberia was feared to be jeopardized and would possibly be negated by future European losses. The fear was real, for in 1512 the nation of Hungary began to suffer defeats at the hands of the Ottomans. Still later, in 1529, the Turks would be at the very gates of Vienna, and all of Europe would be in a panic. It was commonplace for mothers to put their children to bed with the warning that quiet was needed lest the Turks hear and come.

Naturally such calamities, both natural and man-made, turned Europeans to much soul-searching. Indeed, the fevered devotion of the Spanish monarchy near the end of the century can be partially understood in light of such unsettling circumstances. Coupled with this external threat, the papacy itself had suffered greatly in prestige in light of the Avignon detour. The competing popes episode had escalated pessimism about the ability of this person and institution to right itself. The theory of conciliarism, which had surfaced as one solution or at least a better option, had received virtually no support from popes, who were hesitant to share their power. Moreover, as other contests of power between the pope and the monarchs of England and France seemed to show, a new world of political maneuvering seemed now in the making. That is, the emerging reality produced fear or hope that the papacy might not be the most powerful institution in Europe anymore. National forces that until now had generally been weaker than the papacy seemed and were stronger now. Vying with the leaders of nations would grow more difficult for popes.

Moreover, if the papacy found itself in escalating and more intimidating conflict with national powers, not a few of the individual popes of this period found themselves in splendid enjoyment of the Renaissance culture they brought to themselves and their court. Indeed, no small numbers of them were supportive of this culture. To laity and others, they were perceived more as patrons of the arts than, as Gregory the Great had famously described his office—as intended to serve as the "servant of the servants of God."

The point here, however, is not simply that the papacy and the accoutrements of the institution had grown too rich—though some have made that claim. Rather it is that the focus and interests of a pope and Church enamored of these things easily weaken its religious focus. The splendor of the Renaissance replaced the focus of the eyes on the soul. In a word, the worldliness of religious authorities detracted from and weakened their authority. Rather than the authority of the papacy only competing for authority with political leaders of nations, the authority of the Renaissance popes competed with their very office. Little wonder, therefore, that many started to look elsewhere for spiritual direction and order.

However, there was another aspect of the Renaissance in which the impact of that culture would compete with the Church. In the desire of Renaissance thinkers to return to the classical age, many of them became adept at the classical languages, particularly Greek. In the West, once the effect of Irish monasticism had succumbed to the Roman tradition and ties between the East and West had become strained, the West rarely had thinkers who were skilled in the Greek language.

This changed at the time of the Renaissance. Not all who desired knowledge of that language however, possessed the linguistic skill or required tenacity—Petrarch being an example—but others did. In time, able linguists began to evaluate manuscripts, Greek and also Latin. Forgeries were discovered, such as the "Donation of Constantine" by Lorenzo Valla (1407–1457). These new discoveries were of course controversial at the time, but hardly disputable. With this and many other examples, it became evident that the authority of the papacy and the Church may have been given by God, but it came through words and documents, particularly the Bible. Therefore, in an attempt to interpret correctly their meaning, the best effort would fall to the careful analysis and study of grammarians, linguists, translators, ancient historians, and others. Just as to read Plato or Aristotle in their original language required facility with classical Greek, so too, to read the Bible would require facility with the languages in which the Bible was written and more. The authorities on these subjects, therefore, shifted somewhat out of the medieval perspective, but as they did, these new authorities began to offer new perspectives on the world from which they came—the Middle Ages. However, just as the science of Aristotle, which held a predominant sway over the Western world for well-nigh two millennia, began to give way to the new science, the "Middle Ages" would be sidestepped by cultural aspirants committed to a new future for the Western world. With the Enlightenment of the eighteenth century in particular the Middle Ages suffered the most mocking, and it was not until the Romantic Movement arose after that time that thinkers, though mostly literary figures, would look favorably upon the Middle Ages again. It would take later generations of historians to produce evidence for how much indebted to the Middle Ages was the Modern Age.

7

The Medieval Legacy, 1517–1648

PROTESTANT REFORMATIONS

What began as a theological protest with Martin Luther in 1517 would soon divide Western Europe into two hostile factions, Catholic and Protestant, and forever shatter the unity of the previous elusive and fading hopes for a united Christendom. Not for four more centuries, until 1917 and a secular Russian Revolution, would Europe experience another break to match the divisiveness unleashed by the Protestant Reformation. Intended as a reformation of Christianity rather than a division or split, this event initiates and also affirms some existing cultural shifts prompting the medieval into the modern world. Indeed, significant later secular habits and practices are prompted from some originally religious intentions of the Reformation making possible a springboard into secular society later in modernity. Moreover, a century after Luther's protest began, a cataclysmic Thirty Years War, fought from 1618 until 1648, drags the western world closer to a nationalism that moderates the place of religion in modernity. At the conclusion of that war, for the most part, the political or state associations of Protestantism and Catholicism were decided and a limited form of religious toleration among a few differing groups attempted. In addition, the armies of Europe would not again take to the battlefield under overt religious aegis, at least not to the extent witnessed prior to 1648. Often referred to as the "Wars of Religion," the events of these and surrounding decades to a significant degree uncoupled the predominance of religion in medieval culture and substituted the ascendant power of statehood and nationalism in modern culture. The power of the prince, however, in part gained more traction with the Reformation and indeed contributed to some of the successes of the initial Protestants. Such lacing of events and origins ought not provoke surprise, as what is formed is nearly always the result of some things of the past being affirmed even as some components are rejected. The new is virtually never entirely new, for when the future alone is attempted with wholesale rejection of anything from the past, the result of such utopic dream is usually deadly disaster. The Reformation, by contrast, even in its most radical expressions, expressed attempt to remake or realign the Christian Church with some antecedents felt lost or neglected or maligned in the Christian past.

In light of such a consideration, it is entirely appropriate that historians have debated whether Martin Luther (1483–1546) is the last medieval man or the first modern man. To frame the debate in these terms is already to concede that Luther possesses characteristics of both cultural worlds. However, this does not mean that Luther was an indecisive person caught between two ages and who could not decide where he belongs. Luther's eventually famed theological signposts certainly did begin with his pained anxieties over where a sinful man filled with wrong-doing stands with reference to God. Once Luther finds answer to this question in his formulation of being justified by faith in Christ, he in effect reconciles the rightful condemnation by God of sinful men, with the merciful salvation in Christ freely given to men. Luther, however, always the extraordinary but also ordinary man, must continue to battle with himself over the tendency of all to unseat this theological understanding by presuming the good graces of God by their own good works. In this tendency, one might say Protestantism goes against nature, while the life lived as a Protestant at the same time appears to affirm much that is presumed natural about humans as humans. The natural man and the Christian man, for example, takes a wife.

Luther the man is thus far from the prior medieval saint who had typically achieved veneration for a personality and good works and usually miracles that exhibited godly character and calling. By contrast, the so-called earthiness of Luther's personality is often deemed as responsible for much of his appeal—and thus not only as cause for affront to others. Moreover, and again, he exhibited at times a brusqueness of personality that probably endeared him more to ordinary people as opposed to the staid and sedentary scholars from whose occupation and world he had come. Certainly Luther sometimes spoke more for the common man and as unattached from the scholarly man, who of course he was also. Because he gave vent and voice to shared human foibles as well as strong aspirations, his characterizations of his enemies were sometimes very uncouth, such as his characterization of Aristotle as "that damned Greek." However, the effect of much of Luther's life and his teaching and his unadorned "table talk" was to some degree to elevate the layman and the ordinary mortal. Coupled with his Protestant doctrine of the priesthood of all believers, Luther would seem to deserve some credit for elevating the lay life to the previously presumed higher life of the clerics. In addition, the fact that he marries, and marries a nun, appeared as an affirmation of the godly life of the married person lived without benefit of the monastery or nunnery or celibacy. Luther the man glories in marriage as much as he is humbled by the trials of it.

At the same time, Luther would disappoint many initial followers for his hesitations over the aspirations of serfs to rise above the life of oppression, particularly in light of the egalitarian emphasis of the Gospel, as it had been theologically enunciated by Luther. The expectation of many hopeful laity was that the freedom of the Christian man, a prominent title in one of Luther's early and popular pamphlets, would advocate for a corollary social freedom that would unbind them from the chains of other men. However, this aspiration would not happen—at least not with Luther, for Luther was unwilling to couple his desired theological reform to a social reform that might ruinously alter or kill the former for the latter. Acquiescing with the magistrates and princes in putting down a social uprising lost Luther some significant followers, and in part, it also insured that the old political-religious order of the medieval period remained. Later secular thinkers who deem Luther's theological protest much theological ado about nothing would also protest strongly against this beacon light of the Reformation for preferring theological to social justice. It would require other traditions of Protestantism to begin to inch toward theological justification for resistance to tyranny, for example. Typical of a religious age, even one exhibiting some receding of things religious, most all things had to find justification through theological considerations, even wars, and even rebellions against wars.

Luther's initial theological protest was greeted by sympathizers with considerable fanfare, but after a while, the Reformer Luther would be called out by other reformers on theological points. Even during the initial years of Luther's protest, it was becoming apparent that Protestantism might and eventually would fracture. In fact, a colleague named Andreas Carlstadt (1486–1541), who came alongside the protesting Luther initially, began to seriously deviate from Luther in his views of a proper reformation of worship practices to such an extent that the two men permanently broke in their relationship. The central point in much of their disagreement was greater than their own feud, and provoked a significant divide within Protestant worship for the future. It began while Luther was being protected by his prince in the Wartburg Castle in 1521–22. Carlstadt had taken the reigns of reform in Wittenberg and apparently given his assent to much of the destruction of images and icons and statuary that crowds of rioters seemed only too ready to undertake. Condemning such physical actions, Luther strongly chastised Carlstadt for what Luther surmised was Carlstadt's theological nod on the matter. Carlstadt had denied the physical things of Christian worship of any spiritual worth. Luther would charge Carlstadt with spiritualizing Christian devotion with the contestable belief that any and all tangible physical aids to worship were obstacles and blinding impediments from true devotion. For Luther this idea was temptingly attractive for the common man who would tend to dismissively associate the items destroyed with the old social order. From Luther's perspective, all such crowds needed was the blessing and encouragement of a theologian such as Carlstadt who gave theological sanction to their riotous acts.

Indeed, in reading histories of art in the West today, one inevitably encounters historical allusions to such episodes within the Reformation as one sordid affair attributed to Protestant impetus, for in many Protestant villages and countries at the time and later, valuable works of art were destroyed for the sake of religious purity and for fear of idolatry. Whereas Gregory the Great had believed that "Images are the books of the unlearned," here the unlearned destroyed the images for the sake of proper devotion, or as Luther would suggest, perhaps more realistically, out of going along with the crowd. Mob actions were as significant a part of the medieval world as they had been in the classical world. Nevertheless, in Protestantism, images and the like would not enjoy Gregory's justification again. Most Protestants would also lodge complaints against what were deemed many Catholic structures exuding excess and extravagance. By contrast, some Protestant edifices appeared austere to severe. Years later, the Protestant Puritans became known for their preference for the "plain style" and simplicity in form rather than decoration or overt expression. While the medieval Cistercians of previous centuries had affirmed much of this kind of spiritual devotion, in the Catholic Counter Reformation the affirmation of a new architectural style, the busy but luscious and therefore enticing Baroque, was sufficient to indicate the Catholic response to Protestant criticism.

Meanwhile Luther's reservations over desacralizing church buildings and church interiors were met with another notable counter to Gregory by Ulrich Zwingli (1484–1531), who wrote to a friend, "What you give the senses you take from the spirit." The sizeable sector of the Reformation which followed the example of leaders such as Carlstadt and Zwingli oftentimes interiorized the faith, but most always fell short of the mystical inclination, which had few adherents within Protestantism. The religious piety of Protestants insisted upon the interior necessity of things believed without also believing that one found sparks of the divine in the human.

Often historians have suggested that in Western culture Protestantism reengineered the world of church and devotion or piety and work, while giving little time to the pursuits of leisure. Too many days for the saints of Catholic culture was a common complaint of the Reformers. Similarly, the general Protestant attitude toward things like the arts might best be described as unaesthetically utilitarian. By comparison to the medieval world with its stylized Bibles and iconography and statuary and sparkling festivals, Protestantism could look bleaker and more bland. Because of suspicion of art in religious worship and practice among many Protestants, art tended toward the secular in time. From the Protestant perspective, to bemoan such losses was to misunderstand much of its point and impetus. These things had crushed, or at least had laid low, or distracted the human spirit struggling underneath to find peace with God. Protestantism, moreover, could be seen as emancipatory, for it set men free from things which had nearly suffocated them, just as its primary theological understanding freed them of unnecessary mediators, save for the necessary Christ and Christ alone. The iconoclasts of the Reformation, therefore, were not in their eyes grotesquely destroying something beautiful because they despised beautiful things.

During some of Luther's active years, the Swiss reformer Zwingli and he had battled over not a few things, but on the specifics of the Eucharist, they especially clashed. In 1529 the two met at the Marburg Colloquy, debated various theological points, and managed to agree on fourteen, but not on the question of Christ's presence in the Eucharist. Phillip of Hesse (1504–1567), a German prince and early supporter of Protestantism, had hoped to reconcile theological differences in the birthing Protestantism against a rather united Catholic opposition. However, similar to the differences already noted over the place of things physical among Protestant groups so too, the attitudes toward the bread and wine as the body and blood of Christ generally followed the division already noticed between Carlstadt and Luther. Luther remained fairly close to the Catholic doctrine of transubstantiation though he differed in affirming that the bread and wine do remain as such while at the same time contending that Christ is present in body and blood. Zwingli would have none of this in effect double-talk and understood the Eucharist as symbolic of Christ's death and an occasion when the redeemed supplicant recalls and remembers that atoning death. The significance of the Eucharist is in its symbolism and nothing else. There is no magic, no mysticism, and certainly no conversion of wine into blood. The sacramentalism of the medieval period is thus dealt a severe blow with this doctrine, which tended to be embraced by many Protestants, though with the exception of Lutherans and some others. For Luther, such allegiances as he found among his mounting opponents affirmed for him their tendency to forfeit matter for spirit.

Zwingli's early death in 1531 in a one-day military skirmish between Catholic cantons and Protestant cantons at the Battle of Kappel created space for the man most known for marshalling another version of Protestantism outside Lutheranism, called Reformed Protestantism. Though Zwingli was one originator of this tradition, this theological school would soon bear the name of John Calvin (1509–1564), a Frenchman, though much of his life and the notoriety about Calvin, occurred in Geneva, Switzerland. The word "Reformed" is indicative that this version of Protestantism desired to take the Reformation further than its Lutheran antecedents. With Calvin we also reach the second generation of Protestant reformers and the beginnings of an international movement which will spread this Protestant tradition deep within but also far afield of the European continent.

In the history of this Protestant confession, both in geo-political importance and notable cultural accomplishments, this tradition is typically placed high by historians for moving culture closer to the modern age, though oddly so in its "extra" reforming zeal, as indicated by its namesake. Nevertheless, the Reformed tradition of Protestantism significantly etches closer to the modern world in some significant respects. Within the Reformed tradition arises the first, however tentative, Protestant articulation of the rights of citizens to resist and possibly revolt against tyrannical political rule. The intellectual weight of the Reformed tradition places it also in the forefront of educational reforms and in time, economic reforms that advance modern capitalist economies; Calvin's condemnation of the old medieval prohibition against usury was one such catalyst.

While elements of Lutheran worship resembled Catholic worship—despite the prestige of the sermon preferred by Protestants over the Catholic mass—the Reformed tradition tended to be significantly less sacramentalist than Lutherans because of principled cautions against idolatry. The stronger dualism dividing the world of spirit from matter provoked in the Reformed tradition a spirit of inquiry into the secrets of God's world and has been accounted one of the formative conceptual edifices of modern scientific inquiry, coupled with origins from other directives and directions, such as those found in the medieval Franciscan order. Such conceptions prompted more empirical investigation into the workings of nature, as opposed to the broader Catholic notion, where veneration seemed to play a greater role. Equally perhaps, as we approach modernity, the Catholic Church seemed more hobbled to the antiquated Aristotle on science than did Protestants. With the process referred to by historians as "desacrilization," the possibilities for later secular thought can spring into existence. While still regarding the material world as Calvin did as the "theatre of God's glory," in time nature and the laws that govern nature will become detached from God in later modernity.

The ardency of the Reformed spirit and the extension of the Protestant Reformed tradition outward understandably caused Catholic authorities to often assess it as the stronger strain of the variant schools of Protestantism. In part, this reaction issued from quarters of the theological tradition of Catholicism standing against the Reformed doctrine of predestination, but also antagonizing to Catholics was the Protestant Reformed insistence that theological beliefs were determinant of human salvation. As much as this was also a point of Luther, settling on the Reformed tradition as the culprit fitted the ascendency of the Reformed tradition in the Protestant world.

However, theological adversaries sometimes found themselves in union, at least for a time. Against another common adversary both might regard as worse than either of them, both Catholics and Protestants could agree to mutually oppose such an opponent. Into this vulnerable camp fell the despised Protestant Anabaptists, so named for their refusal to regard the inherited medieval belief in infant baptism as a real baptism. With that baptism cancelled out, the need was imperative to be baptized again, but understood because of the inefficacy of the faulty first one. Furthermore, inasmuch as the rite of infant baptism had associations of admittance into both the state or empire and Christianity, virulent opponents of the Anabaptists saw the refusal and denial of the efficacy of infant baptism as tantamount to treason and worse. However, for the Anabaptists, this issue reflected more than when and how many baptisms one should have. That is, because the Anabaptists were hounded ferociously by both Catholics and Protestants in league with the state, Anabaptists argued for the separation of church and state. Their radicalness, moreover, drew them to the keen attention of authorities. When this group of persecuted people had time to think and articulate their objections to the norm in their society, and because they were frequently in hiding and on the run, they esteemed the move made by Constantine, in laying the beginnings of a state and church union, as an experiment and a reality fraught with dangers and especially dangers to the spiritual health of the Church. They of course had much history of the Church at their back to vindicate their point of view. The Anabaptists, therefore, are one of the Reformation proponents of separating the institution and power of the state from that of the Church. Indeed, because of their experience, they regarded a vital mark of the Church as one of being persecuted and this most often undertaken by the auspices of the state. Beyond this idea, moreover, there was another Anabaptist belief—that true Christians could not be proponents or act as agents or officials of the state. St. Matthew might have been a tax collector for Roman officialdom, but should not have been. In their conception, no one truly abiding in Augustine's City of God would be a contributor or employed in the adversary's City of Man. This position necessarily placed this group of people, which would be in time very large as including many of the plentiful groups of Baptists and others, outside the political running of the state.

The theology of the Anabaptists only rarely found its way into print at the time. The steady flow of Anabaptist blood subjugated the flow of ink from this group. The theologians of the movement are hounded to the point that in comparison to the "Magisterial Reformers" such as Luther and Calvin, books are few from their quivering pens because of the frequent need to take flight to avoid capture. A notable exception is Menno Simmons (1496–1561), who bequeaths a fair corpus to his theological offspring and manages somehow to die a natural death. From his namesake, we get the Mennonites. Only in the twentieth century did sectors of this theological culture avoiding political culture reverse the position by coming out into the political world, for fear that the world would be lost if Christians refrained from political involvements. Christians were to bring light to darkness.

THE PROTRACTED ENGLISH REFORMATION

There was another historically important experiment to be tried in the relationship between church and state as a consequence of the possibilities provided for by the Protestant Reformation. Some details of this slice of English history, and particularly those details that include episodes of Henry VIII's multiple marriages, are apt to be known to some readers. However, the consequences of taking the church of a nation away from the universalist auspices of the Roman Church are illustrative of both medieval time and early modern directions.

What Henry (1491–1547) did in England was not completed, we might say, until 1688, when England in effect bulwarked the Protestant foundations of Anglicanism to the satisfaction of most Englanders. However, during the interim decades and even after the Glorious Revolution of 1688, the suspicion of Catholics was at times intense, and consequently there were rare interludes of Catholics living in the safety accorded Anglicans in English society. Moreover, there was sufficient cause from the perspective of English Anglicans for their suspicions of Catholics. Except in the almost single counter instance of the Hussite Church in Bohemia a couple centuries before, no national church had tried and succeeded in breaking free of the Roman Church; for England to undertake such a feat was anything but an ordinary matter. It is comparatively easy then to understand the efforts of the Roman Church to employ virtually every means available to keep the English Christian community within the fold of the Roman Church.

For starters, there was excommunication from the Roman Church which, in the eyes of the vast majority, meant guarantee of perdition, as there was no church outside the Roman Church for one to enlist. What had happened in Bohemia a century earlier was greatly respected in the time of Luther, but remembrance of what had happened to Hus still lingered in the present. Moreover, the nations and nation states around England were Catholic, and some such as Spain, so staunchly Catholic, that even the papacy at Rome let the Spanish Church run most of its affairs from Spain. The Inquisition, now laboring under the most intense work in its history with the menace of Protestantism to contend with, was essentially an affair of the Spanish, run through the order of the Dominicans. Meanwhile, there was also Catholic France, which was another worry for the English to fret over. The English, however, had one religious ally, the Dutch, who in the second half of the century of the Reformation, dared to raise Protestant heads against Catholic princes who seemed prepared to renege on previous promises to concede some political and religious liberties to Protestant citizens.

We are, however, getting too far ahead of our story of Henry VIII, though enough to glimpse the fact that Henry started something in his country that would require his successors to maintain the changes he began. Henry set his nation on a direction which would make England more independent of Rome, though at the same time, England would have to bear the brunt of severe Catholic wrath, which would increasingly in the last decades of the century mean costly wars. In Henry's time and indeed up to much of his daughter Queen Elizabeth's reign, England was short on money, or at least with much less financial reservoirs than nations that presented worries of war for England. Therefore, Henry hardly had the resources to throw his kingly weight around before a European world, the Roman Papacy included. To many observers, England at the time was deemed little more than a European backwater. Indeed, when the Romans left England over a millennium earlier, English life reverted to a primitiveness hardly matched by the ruins of the Empire on the continent. In the interim centuries, England had built little respectable reputation for itself for others to envy. Now things were about to change, however erratically.

For the papacy, some of the English kings had been nearly as difficult to manage as some of the French kings in ages past. Henry VIII, however, in the beginning, had no program for moving his people out of the Roman communion. What he was interested in, however, was having a male heir to replace him upon death. When his first wife provided no such heir, Henry began to consider the possibility of a divorce so as to take another wife and try for the desired son with her. The short and long of this plan, however, was that he required a papal dispensation to do this legally. The Pope might have been willing to grant such a request, if the coterie of European political leaders had not been such a related and extended family. That is, Henry's wife, Catherine of Argon (1485-1536), had a nephew who happened to be the personage of the Holy Roman Emperor, Charles V (1500-1558). The normal ties that bind, therefore, prevented the Pope from conceding Henry's request, and of course, Henry balked and now looked for other ways to pursue his desired course of action. In time and in consultation with his advisors, it was decided that it was an oversight to have asked the Pope, for it was really Henry who controlled, or should control, matters of and for the English communion—so said Henry and some of his circle.

Moreover, and indicative of the magnitude of such a decision, some in Henry's own circle disputed such a move and lost their lives for thinking in opposition to their king. Meanwhile, Henry sires a fair number of future

The Medieval Legacy

rulers, included among them two daughters who will take the throne of their father some years after his death. But indicative of the problems yet to come, one daughter will be Catholic and one will be an Anglican. As a result of Henry's actions England would inherit some tumultuous history after him.

However, when Henry dies, the succession of his son Edward (1537–1553) provides some stability because Edward, though short lived as a king, only ten years, solidifies his father's changes and pushes for more in a greater Protestant direction. Meanwhile, Rome had excommunicated Henry, but with the next head of state, Edward's half-sister Mary, of Catholic persuasion, Rome is pleased, but the transition backward to Catholicism brings back bonfires for Protestant opponents. Mary executes a good number of Protestants, whereas her undiscriminating father Henry had burned both Catholic and Protestant, but much less in number than his daughter. The attribution of "Bloody Mary," moreover, points to the perception of this ruler as prepared to spill all manner of blood if necessary. Indeed, the severity of the Marian persecution sends many Protestants afield, and some of them to Calvin's Geneva, where they become schooled in details and the organization of Reformed Protestantism. After Mary's death and their return from the continent, Anglicanism is infused with Reformed theology because of the exiles' time at Geneva. This theological education hugely contributed to the global reach and influence of the Reformed tradition. Plus, in another half century, England would begin its many seafaring journeys to unknown parts of the world, and would take its religion, however haphazardly, where it went. One more problem, however, was that England's religion was not yet safely decided, even though Queen Mary's successor Elizabeth was not Catholic like her predecessor.

When Elizabeth came to the throne in 1558, stability, religious and otherwise, was direly needed and furthermore, there were abundant troubles across the channel to be given serious attention by the Queen. In addition, because Elizabeth was an unmarried female, the future of England would take on extra anxieties. That is, England's future could be tied to the husband she might tie the knot with and inasmuch as the suitable suitors were largely Spanish or French, that meant Catholic. Something of the same quandary would occur again when Elizabeth's successor, James I, will try for the "Spanish match" for his son, the future king, Charles I. Though Charles did not marry a Spanish Catholic, he did marry a French Catholic in 1625.

As Elizabeth and her advisors would see in the years to come, playing the French and the Spanish off against one another would sometimes be to England's benefit. In any case, and on most every front of problems to confront, these situations still had a strong medieval flavor—religion and religious belief were significantly part of this world. A husband or wife was not just that, and not just a Spaniard or French, for if they were either, they were Catholic. The least anxious union in this period of English history is when in 1688 the English manage to solidify Protestantism in some measure by the marriage of Mary II (1662–1694), raised as a staunch Anglican on the express orders of her uncle, Charles II (1630–1685). William of Orange (1650–1702), her husband, was of Dutch Protestant Reformed lineage.

Protestantism in England, however, had some protections beforehand, and so too had Protestantism on the continent. Despite the superior strength of Catholicism that lay behind the papacy and the Holy Roman Emperor, with the Turkish trouble to the East, opposition to the Protestant heresy never came in sufficient time or strength in the early decades to effectively oppose it. After a while it was evident that Protestantism was in the world to stay. However, and particularly in the next century, an additional fear for Catholics concerned the transport of Protestant heresies from the old to the new world by English and Dutch explorers. In the more immediate present, however, while the Catholic Portuguese and Spanish controlled the seas the problem was not yet as visible as it would be when England began the long legacy of ruling the waves, and became very effective at pirating gold-laden ships of the Spanish.

Even if the Holy Roman Emperor in the person of Charles V had been able to stand down Luther in the most memorable confrontation between the two parties in 1521, Luther and some of his ideas portending the coming world, whereas Charles represented the past. Indeed, Charles, worn out after many burdensome years of dealing with Turks and Protestantism, took to the monastery after abdicating his throne in 1556. However, the monastery would steadily decline in terms of cultural influence, compared to its previous medieval heights. Luther had come out of the monastery to be a married man and thought he had biblical warrant for his decisions on both actions. Luther had the printing press. Of course, so too did the Catholic world, but the Protestants made superlative use of it, just as the Catholic authorities were forming their infamous index of prohibited books and pamphlets not to be read. Perhaps uppermost, moreover, among the factors making the successes of Protestantism possible, were Protestant princes. It was perhaps indicative of the fertility of the Germanic lands for Protestantism over other regions that the Reformation was given birth there, explicitly in Saxony. That is, Protestantism did not have to acquire and maintain the following of a whole nation in the beginning to be ultimately successful. It did require, however, the elector of Saxony, who staunchly defended Luther and Luther's protest. Eventually, however, the Reformation would bring alongside itself whole countries, but what we know as Germany today would not be a whole country for centuries yet to come.

At the same time, it is undoubtable, given an honest view of human nature, that the turn to theological Protestantism was not all or even perhaps most of what turned individuals and particularly princes in its direction. This of course is not to say that man is fundamentally secular man, but that there are plights common to men, princes or otherwise. For the prince, to maintain command or the allegiance of citizens is most assuredly what he considers uppermost in his circumstances. Neither, however, were all princes at the time of the Reformation as thoroughly tactical or cruelly calculating as Machiavelli advised princes in his *The Prince* as early as 1513. What most could not do, for the most part, even if not unflinching opportunists, and in some cases maybe not even close to it, was to put their throne on the line solely for the sake of correct theology. Furthermore, we might say the same for the adversary. That is, for an adversary to consider what to maintain and how to position himself with reference to opposition surely provoked calculations not depending solely upon a theology either. That is, the extant and established Roman communion, which most certainly had and sometimes manifested love of its position and accoutrements, was not governed in its opposition to these Protestant protestors by only a notion of wrong theology, as manifestly wrong as many Catholics thought Protestants were. Indeed, some of the reformers of the high Middle Ages had given the papacy and the Roman Church some glaring comparisons of how churchmen and the papacy might operate toward more spiritual and purer ends. Such groups did not for the most part fare well before their judges nor the people they criticized. Erasmus had been tolerated, but few of his suggestions supplanted the way things were, and later within his own lifetime, some of his books were placed on the Index.

With some political leaders amendable to Luther's ideas, and with the same offering him protection, Luther could stand before the Emperor Charles and not be entirely vulnerable, though of course the entire event and what it was portending was fraught with lethal medieval dangers to the participants. Called upon to retract the essential criticism he had made of Catholic theology, Luther's now famous reply evidences his paramount religious and theological concerns, and important for the coming modern age, his appeal to individual conscience or right that would curry favor in the centuries to come. Luther's appeal was not to human autonomy, but it would provide and make possible a step in that direction. As Luther would contend in his famous paper debate with Erasmus, it was God who was autonomous or free because he was God; the human hardly had a vestige of free will remaining because he was shackled to sin according to Luther. Modern man would of course require and demand his rights as an autonomous individual. Luther in this way would be at odds with the future of Western culture. Said another way, it was more secular individuals of the prior Italian Renaissance who were perhaps the more salient predecessors of modernity and not Luther. Some of the personages of the Renaissance looked like and may have meant to turn away from a world in which religious considerations governed virtually all things. Luther, however, gave a freedom of conscience that further stimulated the push toward modernity.

After the death of Luther, the political concession to Protestantism would come and came to be known as *Cuius Regio, Eius Religio*, and was established by treaty as the Peace of Augsburg in 1555. This treaty in effect gave the state princes of the Holy Roman Empire the right to follow either Lutheranism or Catholicism in their territories. People living in the domain of a prince not of their religious persuasion were given some time to migrate to a more satisfactory region. So now much of Christendom would be broken up into Catholic and Protestant kingdoms and countries. However, to be noted is that no such concession was granted for the Reformed Protestant tradition or any others beside Lutheran. Catholic authorities perhaps viewed the Reformed tradition as the ultimate Protestant nemesis to be held at bay, while grudgingly tolerating Lutherans. This was only the first step of a start toward freedom of religion, however, for real and bloody conflict would lurch into motion as the observance of this particularism would be difficult to abide by after virtually a millennium of not tolerating heretics. Now there were whole lands of them. The Peace of Augsburg was primarily in intent a concession to keeping the peace, rather than any expression that the opponent held a position deserving respect or toleration. The last hope of a uniform Christian society vanished with any such concession. What had happened in 1054 was now happening again after half a millennium, but now happening inside of Western Europe, rather than between East and West.

THE CATHOLIC REFORMATION AND THE WARS OF RELIGION

The wars of religion would be set into violent motion in the next hundred years. The first significant instance of such conflict occurred in the Holy Roman Empire in the area of the Netherlands. Protestantism had gained strength and foothold in some of the northern areas, but political interference by Catholic officials was resisted to the point that some of the Dutch took up arms in protest. The Catholic response was brutal and had the effect of emboldening the independent streak in these Protestant-leaning peoples who now made overtures to the Protestant English for possible aid. Such aid was deemed necessary because the might of the Spanish was not to be taken lightly. Queen Elizabeth, who is known to historians for delaying decisions to the point of maddening her advisors, was hesitant to rouse the ire of the Spanish, who had a much larger military force than that of the English. Part of the problem was that she had factions of her Parliament, to include some of her closest advisors, who felt more strongly about the Protestant cause surviving in the Netherlands than did others. While that position carried some weight with the queen, weightier in her mind was the fear of dreadful consequences from provoking the Spanish, with whom Elizabeth had worked carefully to maintain a tedious peace in years past.

As nations prepared to take to the battlefield for purposes of their religion, or specific religion, it would be easy to surmise that these wars or threat of wars owed their entire existence to the culprits of religion or religious beliefs. If this were so, we might observe fewer such conflicts in ages which manifest more secular than religious motivations. That question aside, as we drew some earlier attention to the motivation of individuals deciding whether to throw their lot in with the Protestants or remain Catholic, so too here, the motivations for the religious wars are multifarious and layered in such a manner as to make an easy dissection and exhibition of all relevant factors nearly impossible. Nevertheless, one might plausibly maintain that historically humans are often prepared to defend their beliefs and not just hold them. That is, the maintenance of a belief in the world, religious or otherwise, may require a defense of that belief, and that belief may require an armed defense to survive. Enemies of course can sometimes be evaded and sometimes appeased, but if the price of non-defense is inevitable defeat, then the stakes surrounding a decision to resist are infinitely high. Thus, aside from some self-interested motives, some of the Protestant world certainly saw the Protestant cause in this light. Without defense, such belief stood ready to be doomed by inevitable destruction at the hands of opponents.

Furthermore, Protestantism had an interest in its own defense, which went beyond theological difference. This was, simply put, a desire to choose one's religious beliefs and accept to some degree the corollary consequences. It is important to note that we have nothing approaching a freedom for religious belief for mere mortals yet, for at this point, and per the Peace of Augsburg, only the prince has that right, and that only in lands of the Holy Roman Empire. For certain other princes, particularly the Protestant ones, the obligation to uphold the people's religion feel squarely on them.

When in 1585 Elizabeth sent English trips onto the continent this triggered the Spanish response of the Armada, which was to come at England three years later. This venture had the blessing of the pope, who was anxious to bring the English back into the Catholic fold. With a huge force coming at her tiny island, Elizabeth had a more frightening worry, apt to be missed if we look at her and her people as too modern. That is, the Catholic Spaniards coming to reclaim the English from their errant Protestantism might count on some English Catholics aiding their efforts. In other words, though Catholic Queen Mary had been unable to sway her subjects back to Catholicism by the time of her death, at least in numbers sufficient for

The Medieval Legacy

them to resist Protestant rule. Elizabeth, however, would hope her people were English enough to avoid recapitulating to a Catholic state. After all, Queen Elizabeth's people had only been Protestants from the time of her father and had swerved away from it for a few years when Mary insisted upon it. What judgment of confidence in her people as a Protestant people could she assume with an undoubtedly superior Catholic and Spanish force coming at her? In other words, as her father and indeed her brother Edward had found, pockets of Catholic resistance were present in this Protestant nation and might erupt as never before to join the Spaniards upon arrival. One worry of Elizabeth was ultimate allegiance; Catholicism might still have sufficient numbers and strength to cripple the English efforts to fend off the Catholic reclaimers. Thus, she waited, but in a huge sigh of relief, found her people with her, and with not a little help from the tumultuous stormy waves of the English Channel. The naval assault in effect never happened because of the weather; the English sent the Spaniards packing in a humiliating defeat. This was not the end of animosities between the two nations, but it seemed to have emboldened the wiry English into undertaking even greater and more venturesome tasks in the future. A question much debated by historians is how much of this accumulating boldness was due to the confidence acquired by a nation after their monarch bucked a religious institution as powerful as the Roman Church. Modern nationalism had won a victory that would be a portend for the future. Shakespeare, Donne, Milton, Johnson, and other notables were just around the corner. A late Renaissance in England still qualified as such and historically proved to be one of the highest peaks of the European cultural world. The backwater country of past ages was being submerged as the English would begin to build the British Empire in this same century.

Meanwhile, Portugal and Spain continued to steer the Catholic course, though not always in happy union. In 1580, Spain managed to subjugate a resistant Portugal as its own until 1640. Even then, it would take the Spanish until 1667 to concede Portugal was independent again. Meanwhile Iberia led the Catholic world, as these nations managed to keep Protestant ideas away so that their peoples barely experienced any exposure to Protestantism. The Inquisition launched from Spain did its work effectively, even as the Spanish Empire began to lose its prior hegemony in Europe in the late seventeenth century. As large as the Spanish Empire was, it was not large or strong enough to do all desired in the new and the old world. Thereafter, France would carry the Catholic mantle, but not without its own internal religious difficulties.

The reverberations of the Reformation in France were of a different kind for the French. Protestantism made significant inroads into France, but never managed to position itself into something of mainstream France for sufficiently long periods. Though anything but a fringe group, Protestants as a French community were nevertheless relatively small but hugely influential. Though English troops had on occasion provided armed relief for the French Protestants or Huguenots, as they were called, the power behind the Catholic French throne was aided in the form of the Jesuit Cardinal Richelieu (1585–1642). Richelieu revealed himself as a politician wearing Catholic dress, and one who was ready to court for political alliance if necessary the very Protestants his order was dedicated to returning to the Catholic fold. Here was yet another example of where politics appeared ultimate, or at least politics perceived as the antecedent and necessary requisite for the victory of the religion. The Jesuit Richelieu was convinced that the Church needed the state. The union of Church and state was never far from his mind.

If the Catholics in Protestant England were most always suspect to the English, the Protestant Huguenots in France suffered immensely greater persecution oscillating with periods of relative peace. However, because the Protestant population in France consisted of many nobles and well-to-do families, so the Protestant strength in France showed itself least in their numbers and more in their abilities and resources. Though vaguely similar to the situation in England in terms of swaying monarchs on various sides of the Catholic-Protestant mantle, in France, the blood-letting was much greater than the years of Bloody Mary in England. On one particular day, August 24, 1572, infamous in French history, the St. Bartholomew's' Massacre laid waste to thousands of Protestants. Nevertheless, because the Protestant back was still not yet broken, the Edict of Nantes in 1598 was issued as something of a concession to reality, and with it, for almost a century, there seemed a possibility that Protestants and Catholics could co-exist together with both being good Frenchmen. Though this act would succumb almost a century later to revocation, for a while it provided a harbinger of the co-tolerance of religions in society that would become a mainstay of later secular states in many lands.

Catholic officials obviously did not want to see their numbers recede because of the advances of the Protestant heretics, and in 1545, the Roman Church convened the Council of Trent. This assembly stayed in session until 1563, with the purpose depicted by various names, usually either the

The Medieval Legacy

Counter Reformation or the Catholic Reformation. Perhaps most notable from these sessions was that Catholics were prepared to concede nothing to Protestant doctrine, as they maintained and expanded upon traditional elements of Catholic theology and practice and worship that would take the Roman Church into the twentieth century. With regard to the front line work of combatting Protestantism, the Jesuits, officially formed in 1540, would be employed as highly skilled soldiers of the army of Christ. The Jesuit founder, Ignatius of Loyola (1491–1556), a Spaniard, had experienced a profound conversion while recuperating as a wounded soldier and afterward took on the mantle of leadership of this famous order. Unlike the older Franciscan order, the new order aimed for influence at the top tier of society, which principally meant political leaders—kings and queens and others of royal rank. Essential to their work was also education and not a few notable modern thinkers, such as the Frenchman Rene Descartes, sat under their tutelage, even as Descartes later lamented the dedication to Aristotle still abiding in their ranks. Among Catholic orders, the Jesuits tended to possess and dispense knowledge at its highest levels. When the Italian Jesuit Ricci (1552–1610) undertook missionary work to China at the turn of the seventeenth century, the mathematician-theologian Ricci took clocks with him to good effect, because the Chinese officials whom he met were very keen to measure time with the greatest possible accuracy. Ricci knew how to impress and how to endear himself to his hosts. Ricci's work and ministry within the Confucian culture of China produced some successes, but with his death, other Catholic religious orders working the same ground objected to some of Ricci's ecumenical methods as too ecumenical. In a very protracted conflict, appeal finally had to be made to the pope for resolution. It would not be the last time that Jesuit tactics would draw eyebrows and judgments from high places.

As effective as Jesuits could be, sometimes they produced intrigues that not infrequently found political leaders tossing them out of a country that had once welcomed them. Even in Catholic Portugal, Spain, and France, they were ousted by 1767. This century of course was the age when secular political leaders or stark nationalism often resented the religious influence of the order and judged the political needs of their states often hindered by the Jesuits. Nevertheless, the indefatigable Jesuits had imbibed the spirit of Loyola who famously published a pamphlet entitled "Rules for Thinking," which cemented the order as one that gave due diligence to unquestioning obedience to superiors. As an example of its dedication to the

Church, one of the rules most quoted in standard histories is that one must believe that black is white if the Church so teaches. Though hypothetical of course, it is illustrative of the degree of devotion required for these servants of the Church. Moreover, just at the time that Protestantism was giving some vent to individual conscience, Catholicism was making renewed pronouncements about maintaining strong lines of authority.

As noted by many historians, Protestantism was at least embryonically positioned for the future, and as we have already noted some elements of Protestantism provided or emboldened tendencies that would only grow in modernity. At the same time, and partly as a result of such factors, Protestantism would also be associated with and sometimes blamed for the turn to secularism in modernity. One example already mentioned suffices to show such a trajectory, however inadvertent the original motivations of Protestant reformers. The Reformed Protestant hesitation about art in churches and Christian worship largely had the effect of pushing art out of religious auspices and into secular venues. Tridentine Catholic culture, however, continued to embrace art in the service of the Church and Catholic worship. For reasons like this, then, Catholicism aided its future, and one strengthened by much of Protestant culture's notable rejection of religious accoutrements that remained needful and popular for many people. Furthermore, the sacramentalism inherent in much of Catholic theology and devotion and practice could indeed retain and also draw converts to Catholicism; devotees could gain succor from the spectacles and mystique of the supernatural and its embeddedness in Catholic life.

Meanwhile, the internecine but armed battles between Catholics and Protestants would continue. Moreover, while the strong Holy Roman Empire continued, the Catholic opposition to Protestantism commanded more troops in the field with tighter organization than the sometimes fickle and often not very unified Protestant states. When a Protestant following became large enough in Bohemia, some Protestants there feared that the emperor could not be trusted to respect the rights of a Protestant prince, as had been affirmed in the Peace of Augsburg in 1555. Thus, the famous retaliation known as the "Defenestration of Prague" in 1618 set into motion a Catholic-Protestant conflict that would precipitate the Thirty Years War. The particulars of this episode of resistance, wrapped in rambunctious behavior, was all out of proportion to its huge political and religious significance. A handful of Protestants tossed some Catholic officials out of a window to a probable, though not actual death, nor even much injury.

The Medieval Legacy

This incident emboldened the Protestant population of Bohemia, and they soon looked for allies who would aid the Protestant bulwark against a sea of surrounding Catholics. For Catholics, by contrast, it was time to reassert control.

A German Calvinist named Frederick (1596–1632), who was Elector Palatine, against the strong advice of his father-in-law, James I of England (1566–1625) and successor of Queen Elizabeth, was persuaded to accept the kingship of Bohemia as a way to unify and strengthen the fewer Protestants against Catholic political neighbors. The Protestant estates in Bohemia had urged Frederick to do so. He consented on August 26, 1619, and was given an expensive and massive coronation November 4, 1619. Witnessing the sumptuous event probably persuaded most that the political strength of Frederick matched his extravagant and expensive coronation. It did not, and such a risky venture necessarily drew the wrath of European Catholic princes, and most importantly, the Emperor Matthias, who viewed the whole affair with disdain and Frederick as a belligerent usurper. The ever savvy Jesuits famously remarked at the time of the coronation that Frederick would be the king for a mere winter; thus, he was dubbed the "Winter King," and his wife, similarly, dubbed the "Winter Queen." Though provided with some money and military to defend the Protestant cause in the Palatinate and Bohemia, Frederick would never receive enough of either for that purpose. Most noticeably lacking from Frederick's paltry resources was the desired support from his father-in-law, King James I of England, who did not wish to rock the boat with his Catholic neighbors any more than it was already tossed.

When it came time for a showdown between Catholic forces and Frederick's Protestant forces, the initial but decisive battle of one day was a portend of things to come for not only Frederick, his forces, and his family, but also for the plight of Protestantism within the Holy Roman Empire. At the Battle of White Mountain on November 20, 1620, some few kilometers to the west of Prague, miscalculations and patchy preparations produced a Catholic rout of the Protestant forces, and Frederick and his family fled in considerable haste. In all probability, the soon-to-be famous French philosopher, Rene Descartes, was in the army of the Catholic Emperor. Modernity was in the making, even as the bullets of the wars of religion flew overhead.

Even after the Catholic rebuke of the Winter King forced a humiliating retreat to the Netherlands, there were further humiliating defeats under the nevertheless highly respected command of the Englishman Sir Horace Vere (1565–1635). Frederick died in 1632, but his wife Elizabeth (1596–1662) and her brood of children managed to hang on to some pitiable semblance of a regal household at The Hague despite their precarious and at times virtually intolerable situation. With Frederick gone, Elizabeth and her top English military officers became a close group, and for some of these English officers, she had immense gratitude and much respect. Given her precarious situation, at times she must have felt they were her only supporters. However, not a few of these officers inclined to Puritanism, and between Frederick's German Calvinism, Elizabeth's own Anglican leanings, and the townspeople who were generally Lutheran, the balancing act was not always easy. Meanwhile, Elizabeth and her officers continued to plead with King James for more financial support for the Protestant cause. It never came: at least not in sufficient quantity.

Moreover, when Elizabeth's brother Charles ascended to the throne after the death of their father King James in 1625, the Puritan impatience with this new king's foreign policy and mounting disdain for his new Archbishop Laud (1573–1645) fomented intractable animosities between both parties, poised sometimes as Puritan and Anglican, with the additional worry about Catholics never far behind. What Elizabeth I had feared might happen during her reign would now soon happen. That is, the religious factionalism within England would soon provoke Protestant divisions within England that would pit Englishmen against one another. The intensity of these animosities propelled much of the human migration from East Anglia in England to the birthing of New England in North America in these same decades. Some of the leadership and investors in these enterprises in terms of the Massachusetts Bay Company and the Virginia Company had first fought—or their fathers or grandfathers—for the Protestant cause in the Netherlands against the Spanish and later as confidantes of Elizabeth, the exiled Winter Queen. Successive generations of some of these families would play a part in the later English Civil War (1642–1651). However, some of the prior familial Puritan heritage would then take the side of the king that most Puritans had earlier opposed loudly in Parliament. Furthermore, for all the failings of King Charles, the Winter Queen could hardly not support her brother in the royalist cause and did.

With the restoration of the monarchy in England in 1660, the English extension to North America escalates, and, as example, the Winter Queen's notable son, Prince Rupert (1619–1682) will, after leading the royalist forces

The Medieval Legacy

for his uncle Charles I during the Civil War, become a founding member of the Hudson Bay Company in present day Quebec. One of Prince Rupert's co-investors in the Hudson Bay Company, Nicholas Hayward, had also invested in land in the colony of Virginia for Huguenots to make homes, after the Revocation of the Edict of Nantes in 1685 forced Protestants from France. The Winter Queen's faithful servant, Lord Craven (1608-1697), is made one of the seven proprietors of the colony of North Carolina by King Charles II (1630-1685). Entrepreneurship now seemed to be one of the most notable Protestant legacies dictating much of the future of modernity.

THE END OF THE MIDDLE AGES

Meanwhile, while some of these actions portended the rise of the modern age, another event, bloody and infinitely protracted, would come closer to closing out the medieval period; this would be the Thirty Years War. This conflict devastated lands in Germany, though precisely how complete the destruction was is still much debated by historians. What is generally not debated is the weariness of Europe with a war, sporadic though it was at times, that not only drug on for three decades, but involved no less than a dozen nations. Historians researching this event encounter document sources in no less a number of languages. Indeed, this war drew in most of the European nations and was perceived by many as a scourge for things past. While England was not a formal combatant, its support of Frederick, and then his wife Elizabeth, kept England close to the struggle.

Modern and contemporary historians have frequently offered their notions of the lesson taken from this War, in terms of what resolution the European powers came to in 1648 with the Peace of Westphalia. For those of a Protestant bent, this conflict provided escape and liberation from the domineering yoke of Catholicism. By extension of this thesis, others have contended that the muddled conflict provided some of the first stirrings toward secular modernity, usually seen as riding upon an advancing nationalism that loosened the religious ties that had previously bound these nations but now had torn them apart. To be noticed, however and historically, is that commitment to the violence of war in the ensuing centuries is scarcely weakened among these nations. However, wars by numbers or extent might recede afterward, because the state now controls and owns, so to speak, violence. That is, as politics becomes increasingly absolutist, for example, political governors issue the times of peace and the times for war of the societies they govern. One might argue, however and with some measure of plausibility, that even if religious identities and confessions recede in influence, these declensions scarcely change the political man left behind. The truth or falsity of positions within this debate to a great degree can be subject to empirical and historical analysis. In other words, though perhaps overstated, political man might modify or find new reasons to fight replacing the old justifications for fighting. Strong religious beliefs, it might be argued, particularly when pushed to the political level, make men strongly combative. Political motivations shorn of religious motivations, therefore, are capable of producing more peaceable men at the political level, or so the argument might go.

One might also consider the extent to which religion and religious beliefs changed location as a result of the Thirty Years War. One might venture with some plausibility that with a lessening of the role of religion in politics, states began to take the steps that eventually produced secular states. This seems to be indisputable to some rather substantial degree. However, more resourceful by way of answer might be to contend that in the aftermath of a war that laid such obvious waste and destruction to so many lives and so much property, settlements achieved without such violence would be preferred more after this war than they had been before. In other words, pulling back might not be so much a pull back from religious beliefs, as a pull back from the destructions of settlements by warfare. However, if there is moderation of the impulses to go to war after the Thirty Years War, this is hardly a concession to secularism as more peaceable that religious societies.

Equally, if not more important to consider, are the ramifications of the birth of science right under the nose of the Thirty Years War. While much has been written by modern historians about the "warfare between science and religion," less has dealt with the intricate complexities of the conflict. The showdown of the Roman Church over Galileo's heliocentric theory of the solar system was certainly one in which the Church saw its position buttressed by biblical considerations, but also by the authority of Aristotle. However, Luther had earlier also contributed his own vehemence toward "this fool Copernicus, who thinks he knows more than the Holy Spirit," in his opposition. But Luther too had frequently appealed to sound reasoning in his disputes with his adversaries, noticeably in his famous "Here I Stand" speech at the Diet of Worms in 1521. One could still plausibly contend, nevertheless, that neither Catholic nor Protestant tradition gave sufficient opening to this widening way of understanding the "new" world. However, the medieval world in great part had substantially provided for, even as it now struggled with, the implications for study of a world created by God. The modern recounting of this struggle usually pits the freedom of autonomy in the modern human against the theological template through which people of the medieval world tended to see all things. If theologians suffered a loss of prestige in influencing political decisions after the Peace of Westphalia, they lost even more in being increasingly shunned or ignored by intellectual currents and thinkers propelling knowledge more in the direction, not just of the secular state, but of a secular and autonomous framework for the study of the world and themselves. The secular template, however slowly, would increasingly set aside both God and belief in the meaning of the human person as previously seen in divine purpose in the Middle Ages. These modern axioms the medieval mind could scarcely comprehend, any more than the modern secular mind can today comprehend the axioms of the medieval mind. One age had birthed another, and in time, the younger would scarcely be able to comprehend the other.

Select Bibliography

Artz, Frederick B. *The Mind of the Middle Ages, An Historical Survey*. 3rd ed. Chicago: University of Chicago Press, 1980.
Aston, Margaret. *England's Iconoclasts*. Oxford: Clarendon, 1988.
———. *Lollards and Reformers: Images and Literacy in Late Medieval Religion*. London: Hambledon, 1984.
Bailey, Michael D. *Fearful Spirits, Reasoned Follies: The Boundaries of Superstition in Late Medieval Europe*. Ithaca, NY: Cornell University Press, 2013.
Bainton, Roland. *Erasmus of Christendom*. New York: Scribner, 1969.
———. *Here I Stand: A Life of Martin Luther*. Nashville: Abingdon, 1950.
Barraclough. *The Medieval Papacy*. New York: W. W. Norton, 1979.
Bireley, Robert. *The Jesuits and the Thirty Years War: Kings, Courts, and Confessors*. Cambridge: Cambridge University Press, 2003.
Boethius. *The Consolation of Philosophy*. Mineola, NY: Dover, 2002.
Brown, Peter. *Augustine of Hippo*. Berkeley: University of California Press, 1967.
———. *The World of Late Antiquity*. New York: W. W. Norton, 1989.
Brownworth, Lars. *Lost to the West: The Forgotten Byzantine Empire That Rescued Western Civilization*. New York: Random, 2009.
Burns, Edward McNall. *The Counter Reformation*. Princeton, NJ: D. Van Nostrand, 1964.
Cameron, Euan. *Enchanted Europe: Superstition, Reason, and Religion, 1250-1750*. Oxford: Oxford University Press, 2010.
Cantor, Norman F. *The Civilization of the Middle Ages*. Rev. ed. New York: Harper Perennial, 1994.
Christensen, Carl. *Art and the Reformation in Germany*. Athens, OH: Ohio University Press, 1979.
Cochrane, Charles Norris. *Christianity and Classical Culture: A Study of Thought and Action from Augustus to Augustine*. Indianapolis: Liberty Fund, 2003.
Coldstream, Nicola. *Medieval Architecture*. New York: Oxford University Press, 2002.
Collinson, Patrick. *The Reformation*. New York: Modern Library, 2003.
Constable, Giles. *The Reformation of the Twelfth Century*. Cambridge: Cambridge University Press, 2002.
Davis, R. H. C. *A History of Medieval Europe*. 3rd ed. Edited by R. I. Moore. Harlow: Pearson Longman, 2006.
Dawson, Christopher. *The Dividing of Christendom*. New York: Sheed and Ward, 1965.
———. *Religion and the Rise of Western Culture*. Garden City, NY: Image, 1958.
Deane, Jennifer Kolpacoff. *A History of Medieval Heresy and Inquisition*. Lanham, MD: Rowman and Littlefield, 2011.

Select Bibliography

Deanesly, Margaret. *A History of the Medieval Church, 590–1500.* Cambridge: Cambridge University Press, 1978.

Dupre, Louis and James A. Wiseman, eds. *Light from Light: An Anthology of Christian Mysticism*, 2nd ed. Mahwah, NY: Paulist, 2001.

Dyer, Christopher. *Making a Living in the Middle Ages: The People of Britain, 850-1520.* New Haven, CT: Yale University Press, 2002.

Eco, Umberto. *The Aesthetics of Thomas Aquinas.* Translated by Hugh Bredin. Cambridge: Harvard University Press, 1988.

———. *Art and Beauty in the Middle Ages.* Translated by Hugh Bredin. New Haven, CT: Yale University Press, 1986.

Foxe, John. *Foxe's Book of Martyrs.* Translated by G. A. Williamson. Boston: Little, Brown, 1965.

Frankl, Paul. *Gothic Architecture.* Revised by Paul Crossley. New Haven, CT: Yale University Press, 2000.

Garver, Valerie L. *Women and Aristocratic Culture in the Carolingian World.* Ithaca, NY: Cornell University Press, 2009.

Giakalis, Ambrosios. *Images of the Divine: The Theology of Icons at the Seventh Ecumenical Council.* Leiden: E. J. Brill, 1994.

Gilson, Etienne. *Christianity and Philosophy.* Translated by Ralph MacDonald. New York: Sheed and Ward, 1939.

Grague, Remi. *The Legend of The Middle Ages: Philosophical Explorations of Medieval Christianity, Judaism, and Islam.* Translated by Lydia G. Cochrane. Chicago: University of Chicago Press, 2009.

Guthrie, W. K. C. *The Greek Philosophers: From Thales to Aristotle.* New York: Harper Torchbooks, 1975.

Hadot, Pierre. *What is Ancient Philosophy?* Cambridge, MA: Belknap, 2004.

Halverson, James L., ed. *Contesting Christendom.* Lanham, MD: Rowman and Littlefield, 2008.

Harwood, Larry D. *Denuded Devotion to Christ: The Ascetic Piety of Protestant True Religion in the Reformation.* Eugene, OR: Pickwick, 2012.

Heale, Martin. *Monasticism in Late Medieval England, c. 1300—1535.* Manchester: Manchester University Press, 2009.

Heather, Peter. *The Fall of the Roman Empire: A New History of Rome and the Barbarians.* New York: Oxford University Press, 2007.

Herrin, Judith. *Byzantium: The Surprising Life of a Medieval Empire.* Princeton: Princeton University Press, 2007.

Huizinga, Johan. *The Waning of the Middle Ages.* Translated by F. Hopman. Garden City, NY: Doubleday, 1954.

John of Damascus. *On the Divine Images: Three Apologies Against Those Who Attack the Divine Images.* Translated by David Anderson. Yonkers, NY: St. Vladimir's Seminary Press, 1980.

Johnson, Paul. *The Renaissance: A Short History.* New York: Modern Library, 2002.

Jordon, William Chester. *Europe in the High Middle Ages.* New York: Penguin, 2001.

Kempis, Thomas. *The Imitation of Christ.* New York: Dover, 2003.

Lawrence, C. H. *Medieval Monasticism: Forms of Religious Life in Western Europe in the Middle Ages.* 2nd ed. London: Longman, 1989.

Luscombe, David. *Medieval Thought.* Oxford: Oxford University Press, 1997.

Select Bibliography

Martin, C. J. F. *An Introduction to Medieval Philosophy*. Edinburgh: Edinburgh University Press, 1996.

Merton, Robert. *Science, Technology and Society in Seventeenth Century England*. New York: H. Fertig, 1970.

Michalski, Sergiusz. *The Reformation and the Visual Arts: The Protestant Image Question in Western and Eastern Europe*. New York: Routledge, 1993.

Miles, Margaret. *Image as Insight: Visual Understanding in Western Christianity and Secular Culture*. Boston: Beacon, 1985.

Ozment, Steven. *The Age of Reform*. New Haven, CT: Yale University Press, 1978.

———. *Protestantism: The Birth of a Revolution*. New York: Doubleday, 1992.

———. *The Reformation in the Cities*. New Haven, CT: Yale University Press, 1975.

Parker, Geoffrey. *Europe in Crisis, 1598–1648*. 2nd ed. Oxford: Blackwell, 2001.

Partee, Charles. *Calvin and Classical Philosophy*. Leiden: E. J. Brill, 1977.

Pelikan, Jaroslav. *Obedient Rebels: Catholic Substance and Protestant Principle in Luther's Reformation*. New York: Harper and Row, 1964.

———. *The Christian Intellectual*. New York: Harper and Row, 1965.

———. *Imago Dei: The Byzantine Apologia For Icons*. Princeton: Princeton University Press, 1990.

———. *The Emergence of the Catholic Tradition (100–600)*. Chicago: University of Chicago Press, 1971.

Pernoud, Regine. *Those Terrible Middle Ages: Debunking the Myths*. Translated by Anne Englund Nash. San Francisco: Ignatius, 2000.

Pieper, Josef. *Scholasticism: Personalities and Problems of Medieval Philosophy*. Translated by Richard and Clara Winston. New York: McGraw-Hill, 1964.

Scavizzi, Giuseppe. *The Controversy on Images: From Calvin to Baronius*. New York: Peter Lang, 1992.

Scott, Robert A. *The Gothic Enterprise*. Berkeley, CA: University of California Press, 2003.

Southern, R. W. *Western Society and the Church in the Middle Ages*. New York: Penguin, 1970.

Stark, Rodney. *The Rise of Christianity*. New York: HarperCollins, 1997.

Stokstad, Marilyn. *Medieval Art*. 2nd ed. Boulder, CO: Westview, 2004.

Underhill, Evelyn. *Worship*. New York: Harper and Brothers, 1923.

Verdon, Timothy. *Monasticism and the Arts*. Syracuse: Syracuse University Press, 1984.

Walker, Williston. *A History of the Christian Church*. 3rd ed. New York: Charles Scribner's Sons, 1970.

Wallace-Hadrill, J. M. *The Barbarian West, 400–1000*. Rev. ed. Oxford: Blackwell, 2004.

Webb, Diana. *Medieval European Pilgrimage, c. 700–c. 1500*. New York: Palgrave, 2002.

Weber, Max. *The Protestant Ethic and the Spirit of Capitalism*. Translated by Talcott Parsons. London: Allen and Unwin, 1930.

Ziolkowski, Theodore. *Modes of Faith: Secular Surrogates for Lost Religious Belief*. Chicago: University of Chicago Press, 2007.

www.ingramcontent.com/pod-product-compliance
Lightning Source LLC
Chambersburg PA
CBHW071444160426
43195CB00013B/2028